HEAVEN UNVEILED

The Amazing Promises of Eternal Life Found in the Bible

Michael P. Clark

someone else so they can enjoy it, too. I'll see you when I come to visit after I leave. I'm not leaving anytime soon.
Love,
Susie M.

ENDORSEMENTS

"You know when you pick something up and read and it immediately catches your attention? A subject like the afterlife can certainly do that! I've known Rev. Mike Clark for many years and I know his heart. I'm so excited that he wrote this book and I'm hoping that many will read it and come to know Jesus even more through it. I have teenage children, 3 of them in fact, and they have so many questions about life, it's purpose and meaning, and what happens after you die. I'm going to have them read this book as I find it to be so helpful to anyone curious about what heaven will be like. Mike is serious about his faith, his love for the lost and his love for the people that have been in his care throughout his career in ministry. I think this book captures all of him as well as his wisdom and knowledge that he's garnered over the many years of study and pastoral ministry. I know you will enjoy it as much as I did and hope you find comfort in knowing that Mike has done the work of analyzing the Scriptures to come to these conclusions. Life in the here and now is much easier knowing that the final destination will be so glorious. May this book be a blessing to you as it was to me."
John A. Terech Jr., Executive Director of Operations
ECO: A Covenant Order of Evangelical Presbyterians

"Heaven - it is the object of some of our deepest longings, as well as the subject of some of our greatest questions. Unknowingly, we allow Hollywood to guide (or better, misguide) our thoughts. Before we know it, we really do believe we become an angel (after all, that's how it is in "The Preacher's Wife"). What we desperately need is clear, simple, biblical guidance. Mike Clark provides the very thing we need in his newest book: Heaven Unveiled. In it he seems to anticipate the questions which so often form in our

heads, but about which we are too afraid to ask. With the heart of a pastor Mike voices those questions for us and then drives us to God's Word to find the answers. Read this book and you will not only have questions answered but more importantly you will find your heart longing to experience heaven yourself."
Rev. Keith Fink, Pastor of Great Valley Presbyterian Church

"Have you wondered what heaven will be like? When does eternal life begin? Who will enter heaven? What bodies will we have? What will life be like in heaven; will it be boring? Mike Clark in his new book Heaven Unveiled answers these and many more questions about eternal life and heaven in a concise easy to read book. Heaven Unveiled is not based on Mike Clark's opinion but on Scripture. Yes, there are rare places where Clark speculates where Scripture is not clear, but even in those few places he bases his opinion on Scripture. Heaven Unveiled offers a wonderful, biblically-based description of heaven that is a must-read for both Christians who have questions about what happens after we die and for people who simply want a succinct view of a central tenet of Christian faith."
Skip Vaccarello, Author of Finding God in Silicon Valley, Silicon Valley Business Executive

CONTENTS

Title Page
Endorsements — 1
Foreword — 4
Acknowledgements — 7
Eternal Daylight Time — 8
Eternal No-Evil Life — 15
Eternal All-Good Life — 25
Eternal Life Relationships — 35
Eternal Life Bodies — 43
Eternal Life Purpose — 52
Eternal Lifestyle — 61
Eternal Life Earth — 69
Eternal Life Dwellings — 78
Eternal Life Rewards — 84
Eternal Life Citizens — 93
Heaven Unveiled Scriptural Appendix — 103
About the Author: — 107

FOREWORD

Myths and misconceptions abound about what heaven will be like for eternity. The most frequently heard misconception is that heaven will be boring. Some picture heaven's inhabitants sitting on clouds and playing harps all day (which, unless you are a harpist, would be terribly boring). This could not be further from the truth, as the Bible does not teach this at all.

C. S. Lewis, an author (who wrote <u>The Chronicles of Narnia</u>) and theologian of great renown in the last century, responded to this misconception in this way *"There is no need to be worried by facetious people who try to make the Christian hope of 'Heaven' ridiculous by saying they do not want 'to spend eternity playing harps.' The answer to such people is that if they cannot understand books written for grown-ups, they should not talk about them. All the scriptural imagery (harps, crowns, gold, etc.) is, of course, a merely symbolic attempt to express the inexpressible… People who take these symbols literally might as well think that when Christ told us to be like doves, He meant that we were to lay eggs."* (<u>Mere Christianity</u>, pg. 120-121)

Another common misconception about heaven, as portrayed by TV shows and movies, is that people entering heaven become angels. That is also not true. The Bible is very clear about what happens in eternal life, and humans don't turn into angels. Many other misconceptions about eternal life abound as well. Along with these misconceptions, people often share many questions and doubts about heaven. Over 40 years as a pastor, as I officiated at hundreds of memorials and funerals, I discovered that most people were confused about the promises of God for eternity. People grieved deeply without much hope for the future. Even regular church attenders often felt that there was little to know about heaven, and that they weren't supposed to know much.

My desire in this book is to bring hope to those who have lost loved ones, ease the tremors of any who fear death, and encourage everyone to live with confidence today because tomorrow brings a greater life in Christ. By replacing the myths with the Bible's truths, hope rises for what awaits after death. I want to share the amazing future for those who trust in God. My family heritage celebrates a greater life beyond. My maternal grandfather explained that he wanted a wake (an Irish memorial party that becomes a celebration of life over death) after he died. I was young when he died, yet that celebration of his life and of his greater future with the Lord stuck with me. It brings me great comfort and peace in the midst of life's trials and troubles. That hope and assurance comes from understanding and appreciating the faithfulness of God to bring about this wonderful and assured future.

We don't have to guess what heaven will be like. The Bible contains far more about what eternal life is like (and also is not like) in the Kingdom of God than most people realize. It is vitally important to understand what the Bible teaches about the truths of eternal life and heaven. In the pages that follow, I made painstaking efforts not to give my own opinions about heaven. My understanding of the truth won't help you because I am not without error and misunderstanding myself. Yet when we have the truth straight from God through His inspired Truth as found in the Bible, we can count on it every time and for all time. There are a very small number of topics where I give some helpful thoughts to some very frequently asked questions about heaven when the Bible is not as clear about them. I note when I do this, but also base these thoughts on the whole of the Bible's teaching. The Bible is where we can find the best answers to our many questions about heaven.

So, in this book I offer an encouraging reassurance that our Lord has the best planned for us now and forever - that we have so much to look forward to and to share in the faithfulness of our Lord. We have so much to live for! This book is not just for those who have lost loved ones in the Lord, it is for all who want to discover the greater joy and life that awaits them as they faithfully follow the Lord. It is my hope that through the pages of this book, you can discover just how grand life will be in that everlasting Kingdom; far greater and more enjoyable than we can imagine. In knowing these truths about eternal life may you be encouraged to draw closer to our Lord in this time, and then to live with confidence that God will faithfully bring everything to a grand celebration on the Day of Christ Jesus for His followers forever.

✼ ✼ ✼

I dedicate this book to the next generation, in particular my grandchildren Colin, Graham, Camille and possibly others yet to come. May you find in this book the knowledge and wisdom you need to look forward with hope and the assurance that many who have gone on before you will be there to welcome you in God's eternal kingdom as you too trust in the great mercy and grace of the Lord Jesus Christ.

ACKNOWLEDGEMENTS

Allow me the personal priviledge of thanking all of those patient friends who took my classes and listened to my Bible messages about Heaven in my last 2 churches.

I am deeply indebted to those who took the time to discuss, read and offer many wonderful suggestions in my thinking and writing about heaven. They brought a much deeper awareness of the truth of Gods' Word than I could have found by myself. There is indeed greater wisdom and strength in numbers of those bonded in love in Christ. I highlight those who gave so much of their time to me. Thanks to the Rev. Keith Fink, who took time out of his busy schedule to help me once again on this book with great theological insights. You keep me focused on the Bible's truth Keith. Thanks to John Terech, who while flying all over the nation, took time to offer so many practical applications and thoughts. I hope those readings gave you some good ways to pass the time on those long flights John. Thanks to Lee Danforth for the fun times we had discussing each chapter. You have such great questions and insights that helped me to clarify the Bible's answers.

My daughters Tricia and Sandra gave me some very helpful suggestions on some tricky questions. I love you both! And my wife Sue provided the persistent encouragement and support to me over 4 years from the beginning of this project when it began as a series of classes then a sermon series that became the basis for the long months of writing this book. My life is the best because of you!

Michael P. Clark, September, 2019

ETERNAL DAYLIGHT TIME

Is There Time in Eternal Life?

Key questions addressed in this chapter:
- When does eternal life begin?
- When is the right time for us to be with Christ?
- Will there be time in the eternal Kingdom of God?

When does eternal life begin? Jesus answered this question directly, giving us a wonderful glimpse into the future Kingdom. In John 5:24, Jesus declared *"I tell you the truth, whoever hears My Word and believes Him who sent Me has eternal life and will not be condemned; he has crossed over from death to life."* Whenever Jesus started a sentence with *"I tell you the truth,"* He meant for His hearers to listen closely because this would be a very important truth. Here He emphatically stated that eternal life begins the moment any person follows Him as their Lord and Savior. It does not start when a person dies. Eternal life begins in this life on earth when we believe in Him, meaning trusting Him with our life and future. Think about this. Wherever you find a king, you also find his kingdom. Wherever the President of the United States goes, all the authority and representation of the United States goes with him. He flies in Air Force One, the presidential plane. He speaks with the seal of the president in front of his lectern. The flag of the United States flies behind him to his right. Even more so, wherever we find Jesus, the King of Kings, we find the Kingdom of God represented and present. The more we learn to follow Jesus in this life, the more we understand and experience the eternal Kingdom of God. And in the presence of this experience, its majestic and powerful influence begins to transform us into eternal Kingdom citizens.

Then, said Jesus, eternal life continues after death, as death has been conquered by Jesus for His followers. We have already- *"crossed over from death to life."* Death will not be the end. Death will be a passageway to the eternal Kingdom. We walk through the valley of the shadow of death with the Great Shepherd Jesus to continue eternal life with Him beyond.

Life with Jesus gives us glimpses of what to expect in eternity. The life He demonstrated while living on this earth, and the life we experience living on this earth with Him, displays some of the greater life we can expect in the eternal Kingdom of God. For Jesus, eternal life is one and the same with the abundant life He came to share. He proclaimed this in John 10:10 *"I have come that they may have life, and have it to the full."* Eternal life is abundant life in Jesus; life to the full – meaning complete, satisfying, rich, plentiful – the exact opposite of boring, dull and dreary life. Jesus brings life full of love, joy, peace, patience, kindness, goodness, gentleness, faithfulness and self-control (Galatians 5:22-23). Those adjectives describe the lifestyle of the people of heaven; the lifestyle lived fully in the Kingdom of God. Jesus healed every illness brought to Him, defeated every evil He encountered, and banished death from every funeral He attended. That is what we can expect in the fullness of His kingdom – no illness, evil or death. Jesus brings wisdom, glory and power for all who believe in Him for eternal life. We have so much now and forever to experience in life with Jesus.

Maybe you wish we could be with Jesus fully now. You might ask "Why wait to be with Him in the eternal Kingdom? Why doesn't God just beam us up today into that place? Why do we have to wait to join Jesus there?" The Apostle Paul wrestled with these questions too. He answered the question "When is the right time for us to be with Christ?" In Philippians 1:21-24 Paul wrote (NIV) *"For to me, to live is Christ and to die is gain. If I am to go on living in the body, this will mean fruitful labor for me. Yet what shall I choose? I do not know! I am torn between the two: I desire to depart and be with Christ, which is better by far; but it is more necessary for you that I remain in the body."* I can understand Paul's conflict. He faced a lot of suffering and trials as an Apostle for Jesus. He experienced many hardships and listed some of them in 2 Corinthians 11: persecutions, bad health, 3 shipwrecks, harsh cold, court trials, and imprisonments. He was almost killed several times for following Jesus as he endured 5 intense floggings of 39 lashes, countless whippings of other sorts, beatings and stonings from those who opposed the message of Christ. The enemies of Christ eventually beheaded Paul. He knew suffering and agony in this world, so he longed to be with Christ in His eternal Kingdom where none of that suffering would ever occur.

After death, Paul knew that life with Christ in the eternal Kingdom would be much better than life in this world. Yet he also knew that the Lord called him to share the great news of eternal and abundant life with Christ with those who also needed to hear and receive it. Which would be granted to Paul: the greater eternal life with Jesus or the present and vital ministry for Jesus? It seems that Paul could choose to ask Jesus to take him from this life; but Paul also knew how important his ministry was for those he served. To find the answer Paul trusted that decision to the will of the Lord. We face the same dilemma with the same faith. We know that the eternal Kingdom will bring us amazing love and joy forever without any pain and sorrow; but we remain as long as we can to be helpful serving others in the Lord. When is the right time to cross over through death to eternal life? We trust the Lord to answer that question for us, just as Paul did.

We know that the Lord has every day of our lives numbered in His greater will for us. This means that we will not go to that Kingdom one day or even one minute sooner or later than we should. This is a very comforting truth. When we die in this world, it will be the right time for us to make that journey to our true home. Two verses make this truth very clear: Psalm 39:4 (NLT) *"LORD, remind me how brief my time on earth will be. Remind me that my days are numbered— how fleeting my life is."* And Job 14:5 (NLT) *"You have decided the length of our lives. You know how many months we will live, and we are not given a minute longer."* God knows exactly the length of our lives, so we don't have to be anxious about tomorrow or about our deaths. Our effort is to be focused about today. Jesus said it this way in Matthew 6:34 **(NIV)** *"Therefore do not worry about tomorrow, for tomorrow will worry about itself. Each day has enough trouble of its own."* We start eternal life with Jesus by believing and trusting in Him. We learn how to live with Jesus by following Him day by day in this world. Then, one day Jesus will take us through death (or by His return) into the eternal Kingdom so that we can experience the fullness of life with Him forever.

What will that be like? Will we have days and nights, months and years when we live eternally? Will there be time in the eternal Kingdom of God? The Apostle John gave us insight into this interesting question in the Book of Revelation. Revelation 22:1-5 **(NIV)** *"Then the angel showed me the river of the water of life, as clear as crystal, flowing from the throne of God and of the Lamb down the middle of the great street of the city. On each side of the river stood the tree of life, bearing twelve crops of fruit, yielding its fruit every month. And the leaves of the tree are for the healing of the nations. No longer will there be any curse. The throne of God and of the Lamb will be in the city, and His servants will serve Him. They will see His face, and His name will be on their foreheads. There will be no more night. They will not need the light of a lamp or the light of the sun, for the Lord God will give them light. And they will reign for ever and ever."*

Look for the interesting facts about time and the Kingdom of God in this passage. Notice that it is always day in God's Kingdom, as sun and lamp light are not needed in the brilliance of God's presence. God is light! (1 John 1:5) No darkness can exist in His presence. Jesus is also the Light (John 8:12) There can be no night with God. We can consider this in two senses. On one hand, we can take the passage literally. If there is no night, there is no need for other lights, and, therefore no need for the stars, moon or sun. The other possibility is to take this passage symbolically; to say that darkness is where evil hides. Since God is always present and no darkness or evil can be in His presence, this verse then would mean there is no evil in the eternal Kingdom. Revelation 22:1-5 certainly means that there is no evil there, as we will more fully explain in the next chapter. But it also conveys the truth that God never sleeps and that God is Light. He cannot be anything other than full light in all His radiant being. This passage refers to the Holy City in which God will make His throne as a specific place. Maybe the rest of the world will have some night, and the stars and moon will exist somewhere? (We will address that question in a later chapter). But this much is clear: in God's presence there is no night and no darkness at all.

Does this mean that without nights, we will not sleep? Does this mean that without nights there will be no division between the days and thus no time in the eternal Kingdom of God? Life with God presents some very unusual circumstances. Humans are finite beings created to live in specific dimensions of space and time. God lives outside of human, natural, spatial dimensions. The theory of relativity $E=MC^2$ reveals that if something exists at the speed of light, that something would be of infinite mass and time would stand still. As light He exists in this infinite dimension. The measures of height, width, length, volume, speed, hours, days, months and years do not apply to God. He lives outside, above and beyond these dimensions. So, how do finite creatures live with an infinite God? That is one of the great questions about living in the eternal Kingdom. Humans need places to live, relate, play, work and do all that humans do. God does not require any of these places. Humans need time and space as created beings. God does not.

So how does it work? Is there space and time in the eternal Kingdom lived with the infinite God? Yes, there is. Jesus already demonstrated that the eternal, infinite, unbounded God can live with us in our dimensions. God enters into human dimensions, but humans can't live in God's unlimited dimensions. Humans need and will have space and time in the eternal Kingdom. Remember, eternal life means life has no ending, not that it has no beginning or time. We have a beginning in our birth. We have time to live with God and each other. While there may not be nights in the eternal Kingdom, look more closely at the first verses of Revelation 22 and see that time is mentioned there. (NIV) *"On each side of the river stood the tree of life, bearing twelve crops of fruit, yielding its fruit every month."* There are months in the eternal Kingdom! Months need days, and months add up to years. There is a measurement of time, so time will exist. Humans of the eternal Kingdom will live day by day, month by month and year by year.

Maybe this suggests to you that eternal life will be non-stop busy with no time for rest, relaxation or fun? No, don't get confused by our life and time here. There will be no 'busy' in the eternal Kingdom. There will be no stress from too much to do or too many expectations to meet. Time will take on a new character for God's people in the eternal Kingdom. Time was set in the Garden of Eden as good for humans before the Fall, and so it will be again in eternity. In this world, time was corrupted along with everything else when humans failed to live in obedience to God's perfect timing and will.

In our present existence on this earth, there are two types of time as described by 2 Greek words: 'kairos' time and 'chronos' time. 'Chronos' time is the time of seconds, minutes, hours and days that keep moving forward with each tick of the clock. When we live without God's wise direction, we misuse this time; wasting and losing precious hours and days by doing things that are not good or important. Doing these things, we get overwhelmed, busy, stressed and frazzled. 'Kairos' time is the 'right' time when everything falls into place and all gets done that should get done. In 'kairos' time, nothing is rushed or prolonged. Those living in 'kairos' time find all the time they need in the right place to accomplish all good things needed to be done. 'Kairos' time brings the balance of life as the Lord helps us to reorganize our priorities and use our time wisely. In the Lord's time ('kairos' time'), we discover that balance of using the time we have for the good things He has in store for us.

In the eternal Kingdom, people will not waste or lose time but use it wisely in full compliance with the will of God. There will be all the time needed for all the good things to enjoy and thus to find meaning in this perfect time. 'Kairos' time will merge with 'chronos' time, so all can live life full, balanced, whole and complete in the Lord. We will have time for it all – all the life we could ever dream of or imagine – life full of wonder, meaning, joy and love. (And by the way, people won't get tired either, so they will have all the energy they need to do all the good things. But I will write more about that later.)

To close this teaching of God's Word about eternal life, let's sum up what makes this all so amazing and possible. Eternal life will not be eternally dull, boring, tedious or drag on and on. Eternal life will be abundant and full. Why? Because eternal life is all about living forever with Jesus. He empowers us to enjoy an incredible, life-in-all-its-fullness, abundance. The Apostle Paul said it perfectly *"For me to live is Christ and to die is gain!"* The more we learn in this world the priceless meaning of that phrase to live with Christ every today, the more we can look forward to tomorrow and eternity with Him. Jesus makes all the difference for greater life. He always has and always will bring life to the full. Will you trust your today and your tomorrow to the One who is the Way, the Truth and the Life? I hope you will.

ETERNAL NO-EVIL LIFE

Life with the Absence of Evil, Suffering and Chaos

Key questions addressed in this chapter:
- What will life be like in heaven where there is no evil?
- How can there be diversity in heaven without division and conflict?
- Will there be any suffering or pain in heaven?
- Will people be capable of and willing to do wrong in heaven and thus harm it like humans have done on earth?

Eternal life is not so hard to understand. Our misconceptions about heaven can be removed and much of our confusion cleared up. So much about eternal life has already been revealed by Jesus and the Word of God found in the Bible. The people of the eternal Kingdom of God will not be angels but will be sons and daughters of God. They will not be bored, because they will enjoy the fullness of life found in Jesus. We look forward to the promise of a very bright eternity.

If we desire to understand eternal life, many glimpses of it can be found in an unexpected place, the beginning of humanity. How God created humans, as described in the Book of Genesis, reveals His intentions for humans for eternity. The Fall, when humanity turned away from God and did things not good for them, corrupted much of this life with God. This corruption of life included the loss of eternal and abundant life. God created humans to live with Him forever. Death came as a consequence of the Fall to stop this eternal life for a time. Much like an electric light or television stops working when the electricity fails, so humans decay toward death when their God source of life gets disconnected. However, Jesus, the One who is the Resurrection, brought back eternal life with God. He will also bring back that Garden of Eden experience for humanity's delight. In that paradise, there was no evil, suffering or hardships, and so it will be for eternity. That is our key topic for this chapter - eternal, no-evil life. So, what did that life look like back in creation, and what does that tell us about our future life?

The first verses of Genesis (1:1-2), filled with many great truths, reveal a very important truth about God. (NIV) *"In the beginning God created the heavens and the earth. Now the earth was formless and empty, darkness was over the surface of the deep, and the Spirit of God was hovering over the waters."* You may have heard the saying that nature abhors a vacuum. Well, God can't stand a vacuum either; not when it comes to bringing the fullness of life to humanity. Wherever God finds emptiness, He fills it with substance. When God meets formlessness and chaos, He brings harmony and order. And God always overcomes darkness with light. (Even what we consider to be the dark, empty reaches of space become the playgrounds and passageways of the unseen eternal creatures that attend to God.) This was true in the beginning of the earth. It is true now in our lives with Him. It most certainly will be true in eternal life with God. God creates, organizes and radiates every place and person He touches. Do you have places of emptiness, chaos and darkness in your life? Let the Lord bring His life, harmony and light into them. In the eternal Kingdom of God, there will not be one stray atom to ruin God's harmony. No speck of darkness can abide His brilliance. His holiness eradicates every trace of evil.

Just as God designed incredible diversity of life forms to fill the air, water and lands of the created world, so again, our wondrous Creator God will populate His new heaven and earth with a greater, wondrous, diversity of life. Yet, maybe more amazing, is the fact that all this diversity lives together in perfect peace. Nothing harms another thing. None will bear ill will or cause division. All co-exist in harmonious and complimentary life. Examine the Garden of Eden to discover this truth. It contained no weeds or poisonous plants. Its plants had no thorns to inflict pain. All the many plants yielded an abundance of fruit and produce. The work of those first inhabitants of this paradise included only keeping those plants pruned so they would not overwhelm everything in their lush growth. Like God, the first humans worked to enhance the garden by checking the chaos with order, by promoting harmony amidst the diversity, and by letting life flow out to fill the emptiness. It was all good for humans, for creation and for God. This abundance of good signifies the intention of God for future life with Him; a life without darkness, emptiness or chaos, yet full of light, diversity and harmonious order. The citizens of heaven will work again at promoting harmony in the abundant diversity from God in a land where there are no weeds, thorns, poisonous plants or any other harmful thing.

The Old Testament provides many glimpses of eternal life with God despite the problems created by turning from God. We read of those problems in Genesis. In just a few generations after the fall of humanity, evil filled the earth again with chaos, darkness and death. The first son murdered the second son. Clans and gangs formed. Battles broke out. Humans invented new ways to slaughter one another. After all this trauma and terror, the prophet Isaiah gave a great hope for the future in describing what happens when God brings peace between nations and peoples. Isaiah 2:4 shares this peaceful vision of eternal, no-evil life. *(NIV) "He (God) will judge between the nations and will settle disputes for many peoples. They will beat their swords into plowshares and their spears into pruning hooks. Nation will not take up sword against nation, nor will they train for war anymore."* No war, military, or combat equipment will be needed in the Kingdom of God. No swords or guns will be found there - no spears or grenades, chariots or tanks either. No one will train for war or attack each other. All the energy and resources humanity once devoted to defense and annihilation become free for pursuits of health and fulfillment.

Wouldn't it be nice if we could take the trillions of dollars the world's countries spend on military defense and use it for better things for all? We could have smooth roads, safe bridges, modern hospitals and schools, fun playgrounds for children, new national park facilities, eradicate hunger and poverty, and provide plenty of research money to find cures for illnesses and maladies of all kinds. A people freed from worry about war can do amazing things. That brings great hope in looking forward to this absence of evil in the eternal kingdom of God. We won't need locks on our doors, alarms in our cars, homes and offices, or insurance policies. Police and fire officers, lawyers and judges will need to find other jobs. All our efforts every day will be directed toward greater life, not lesser life.

This greater life also excludes all suffering, sickness or sadness. Revelation 21:4 makes this fantastic announcement about eternal, no evil-life with the Lord. **(NIV)** *"He will wipe every tear from their eyes. There will be no more death or mourning or crying or pain, for the old order of things has passed away."* Can you imagine life without disease, deformity, handicap, imperfection, weakness, infirmity, plague, coughs, colds, flues, headaches, aging and all that go with them? There will be no suffering, grieving, sadness, depression, death or pain of any kind in God's Kingdom. There will be no need for doctors, nurses, medical technicians, police, fire, emergency personnel, mortuaries, cemeteries, or any occupation that deals with suffering, wrong or death in any way. How would your life change if you never had to worry about getting ill or suffering? Every waking thought will be freed from anxiety and grief, so we can be focused on love, joy and peace with God and each other. This is the eternal, no-evil life those who trust in the Lord can, with assurance, look forward to forever.

When humanity throws off the chains of slavery to wrong, evil and injustice, then we can finally live freely as the Lord intended. This includes no longer having to deal with Satan and his demonic forces that lie behind the evil we face each day. The Apostle Paul told King Agrippa that his call from the Lord (Acts 26:18) was to carry out this freeing ministry. (NIV) *"I am sending you to them to open their eyes and turn them from darkness to light, and from the power of Satan to God, so that they may receive forgiveness of sins and a place among those who are sanctified by faith in Me."* As followers of Jesus share about the Lord, they share Paul's call to open eyes, turn people from darkness to light, and release them from the power of Satan to God in forgiveness for eternal life. The final end of Satan and the demons is revealed in Revelation 20:10 (NIV) *"And the devil, who deceived them, was thrown into the lake of burning sulfur, where the beast and the false prophet had been thrown. They will be tormented day and night for ever and ever."* On that day, no evil will ever again exist in God's eternal Kingdom to mar or spoil any portion of eternal life with God.

Yet, there is one more concern to address in this chapter. What about the followers of Jesus? Even though they follow Jesus now, there still exists within their nature the potential to ruin life forever. They are still capable of doing wrong and harming each other. Like a latent disease germ living in an unaware or unable to be healthy individual, must followers of Jesus be quarantined from God's Kingdom so they won't bring in the concealed evil within themselves? How can anyone hope to live in the eternal, evil-free kingdom if that evil still resides within their desires and thoughts? Even though we would like to think we are selfless in Christ, we remain selfish in our desires. Even though we don't commit adultery, we still contemplate it. Even though we don't murder, we still harbor life-ending thoughts about others. Even though we think we are kind, we catch ourselves too often harming others. We need a change of mind and desires, a freedom from our moral imperfections, or we will ruin the hope of a no-evil, eternal life.

The answer to this is found in the final work of Jesus called 'glorification' that is yet to happen for His followers. A key verse to understand glorification is Romans 8:30 in which the Apostle Paul reveals the completed work of the Lord for His people. **(NIV)**

Michael Paul Clark

"And those He predestined, He also called; those He called, He also justified; those He justified, He also glorified." Without getting into several other key theological truths contained in this verse, let's focus on the concept of the work of Jesus to glorify His followers. Briefly, we can list 4 Biblical states of humanity in regard to right vs. wrong and goodness vs. evil that lead eventually to eternal, no-evil life in Christ.

First, humans were created in innocence. The first humans lived whole and healthy lives of integrity. They walked unashamed before God as they did no evil or wrought corruption through wrong. They could be in His company in that innocent state. However, they were also capable of choosing to do wrong and disobey God. Don't get confused about this. God did not create them to do wrong but to always do right. God did not give them a choice to do wrong, as some erroneously believe. Free will is not about choice between good and bad. Free will is the complete freedom to do right. A free will is a will not enslaved to corrupted thoughts. A free will is not limited by perverted desires and addictions. A free will enables a person to what is best for herself or himself. Natural limitations on human existence do not affect free will. Every creature has some limitations on its existence as it was created by God. A fish cannot live out of the water but lives freely in the water. A bird cannot live in the water but can soar freely in the skies. God designed humans to live freely in the Garden of Eden (not in the water or in the air but on the land) under God's reign. They had free will to live as they were created. I did not give my children the choice to disobey my instructions concerning using knives or medicines when they were little. They were simply not allowed to use them out of concern for their safety. When they were old enough, I taught them how to use knives and medicines safely for good. So, God did not give the first humans the choice to eat of the Tree of the Knowledge of Good and Evil. He told them they could not eat. It was bad for them to do so. There was no choice offered. Only one thing was required and that was to trust God in what was right. Maybe later He would have shown them how to properly use the fruit of that tree, However, in their immaturity God forbade the first humans from eating that fruit. They had free will to do what was right and enjoy life fully as they were created by God.

Adam and Eve lost their free will, their ability to live innocently in God's presence, when they disobeyed Him. In their disobedience, humanity fell into the 2nd state of corruption or depravity. In this state humans are certainly able to do wrong, but they have a hard time doing right, rarely achieving it. Humans quickly descended from the good of the garden to the evil of darkness and death. This fall corrupted every part of human life. What we think is good, is a mere shadow of what God intended for our good. Darkness inhabits and inhibits every thought and action humans have in this state of living without God. Hatred, war, enmity, jealousy, murder, theft, selfishness, and so many other dehumanizing behaviors became rampant upon the earth as symptoms of this fall from humanity's created innocence.

However, God would not let His creation remain in this darkened, hopeless state of corrupted evil. He sent His only Son Jesus to bring light, life and right back among humans. He lived among humans to reveal His right life, died for all to take away human wrong life, and lived again for any to follow Him to the eternal right life - no-evil life. All who trust and believe in Jesus as their Lord and Savior receive His abundantly good life. This is the 3rd state of humanity, but it is only found in true followers of Jesus. They are justified in Jesus' righteousness; meaning they are forgiven and cleansed of their record of wrongs and evils. In this justified state in Jesus, His followers become again capable of doing right by the power of His Holy Spirit, yet they also remain able to do wrong by denying and grieving the Holy Spirit. Followers of Jesus can begin the process of sanctification – the cleansing of the Holy Spirit – in this life but can only get so far. Residues of evil, the bad habits that remain in their thoughts and desires, can still lead them astray. Yet, the more Jesus' followers rely upon the leading and cleansing power of the Holy Spirit in their daily lives, the more He can work among them to bring healing in their lives and glory to God. The Apostle Paul described how this work of sanctification has begun already in the lives of the followers of Jesus. 2 Corinthians 3:18 (NIV) *"And we all, who with unveiled faces contemplate the Lord's glory, are being transformed into His image with ever-increasing glory, which comes from the Lord, who is the Spirit."* This is a process for followers of Jesus as they "*are being transformed*" to become like Jesus in healthy, wonderful life.

In this present world, followers of Jesus can only begin to experience the glory of living in the Lord's image. Much more is needed to eradicate any thought and initiation of wrong doing. Perfection in living without any wrong behavior is needed for heaven. Thus, followers of Jesus need the 4th and final work of Jesus to bring them to this moral perfection. This final work is the complete glorification of life that occurs on the day Jesus takes them into His eternal Kingdom. In this fourth and final state of full redemption, followers of Jesus always do what is right and never desire to do wrong. Every thought and action will be only for the good and glory of God all the time. This is the state of complete maturity in Jesus when His followers become fully like Him in their moral lifestyle. No thought of disobedience or desire against God's good, perfect and pleasing will ever enters into the minds and hearts of the glorified in Christ. If they could have such thoughts and desires (which they will not), they would become totally disgusting and abhorrent to them. They will not entertain them as they will not want to carry them out in any way. They cannot be tempted to sin or wrong. When I was young, I liked sugary cereals that now, as an adult, I don't want to taste again. When I was a teenager, I enjoyed silly TV shows such as "The Monkeys" or "Batman" (that dates me). I have no interest in watching those shows again as an adult. Even more so, in the state of glorification by Christ - the full maturity His followers enjoy in Christ in His eternal Kingdom - they will not desire or think to entertain any wrong or evil desire.

By the way, this is the only perfection Jesus' followers will experience in eternal life. They will be morally perfect so that they won't do any wrong, cause any hurt or spoil eternal life in any way. They won't be perfect in other ways, just morally. They won't have all knowledge, so they can keep on learning. They won't be perfect in power, so they can keep on trusting in God. In other words, they won't be gods as some erroneously suggest. They will be amazing kingdom creatures, just as God created and intended each of His followers to be as fully human beings.

When does this glorification happen? The Apostle Paul answered that question in 1 Corinthians 15:51-52 (NLT) *"But let me reveal to you a wonderful secret. We will not all die, but we will all be transformed! It will happen in a moment, in the blink of an eye, when the last trumpet is blown. For when the trumpet sounds, those who have died will be raised to live forever. And we who are living will also be transformed."* The transformation Paul wrote about is the glorification that occurs when those who have died with Jesus will be raised forever as sinless, evil-free citizens of God's eternal Kingdom.

I wrote in the last chapter about one of my life verses, Philippians 1:21 (NIV) *"For me to live is Christ and to die is gain!"* We are to live every day in Jesus presence to learn to live in His abundant life for us today and forever. Now, I will share my other life verse, Philippians 1:6 **(NIV)** "...*being confident of this, that He who began a good work in you will carry it on to completion until the day of Christ Jesus."* This is the assurance of the promise of glorification in Jesus. He worked to justify His people on the cross. He lives with them now to sanctify them for cleansing to holiness. He will also finish His work to bring them to completion, to full maturity in glorification. This is the total living without any evil in full goodness state of glorification, so they can live once again in the presence of God the Father. This is eternal, no-evil life.

Next chapter, I will describe what it means to have eternal, all-good life. I hope you begin to imagine what that will mean for an incredible and abundant life forever.

ETERNAL ALL-GOOD LIFE

Life with Every Good of God

Key questions addressed in this chapter:
- Will we recognize and know loved ones and friends in heaven?
- Will there be animals in heaven?
- Will people remember their failings and regret them forever?
- Will they remember the failings of others and condemn them in heaven?
- What does it mean to have the full mind of Christ in heaven?

Talking with some people about eternal life, I hear their fear that heaven will be less than what they hope it will be. They question if they will recognize loved ones, if animals will be present, or if eternal life will be enjoyable and productive. We can put to rest all such concerns because the Bible answers them clearly. I will address this in a general way and then tackle each concern in more specific ways. The next level of life with Jesus is not limitation but expansion, not loss but gain, not diminished but abundant life. Humans enjoyed great life in the Garden of Eden. We lost that abundance when we turned away from God and cut ourselves off from Him. Jesus came to return humans to the abundant, joyful life with God that is so much more than we can imagine. Followers of Jesus gain more than was lost in the fall of humanity when they follow Jesus into His eternal Kingdom!

We fear the future because of the losses we experience in this darkened and corrupted world. We fear the future because we have known so many disappointments. We don't want to build up our hopes because we have been let down in so much sorrow and grief. Don't let the darkness and confusion of this world with all its fears and misconceptions keep you from the assurance of a greater future with the Lord. I repeat, all those who follow Christ will gain back the humanity that was lost and more. Jesus sets them free from their wrongs and sinful inclinations, so they can live freely for greater life in Him. The more we know the King, the more we experience His Kingdom; especially as we will know Him fully in eternal life. Therefore, look forward to what will happen. That future life will be much greater than we can imagine, not less.

The Apostle Paul wrote about this wondrous, greater life we look forward to embracing in 1 Corinthians 13:8-12. (NIV) *"Love never fails. But where there are prophecies, they will cease; where there are tongues, they will be stilled; where there is knowledge, it will pass away. For we know in part and we prophesy in part, but when completeness comes, what is in part disappears. When I was a child, I talked like a child, I thought like a child, I reasoned like a child. When I became a man, I put the ways of childhood behind me. For now we see only a reflection as in a mirror; then we shall see face to face. Now I know in part; then I shall know fully, even as I am fully known."*

In these verses, Paul gave two illustrations of how our lives with the Lord will expand beyond our present circumstances. First, he shared that we understand like children now, then we become fully mature in the understanding of eternity. What seems so mysterious will become quite reasonable. Paul referred to the 'mirrors' of his time. Those mirrors were not anything like our highly reflective mirrors of today. Those mirrors were polished metals that returned an obscure and twisted reflection of faces, not a clear reflection. Using these old mirrors as a metaphor, Paul wrote that we see dimly now into the future, but will see with detailed clarity in the amazing eternal life with God. Have you experienced one of those "Aha!" moments when you suddenly understood something you tried so hard to grasp? A time when you were so confused, but suddenly everything snapped into place and you understood it clearly? I told my grandson a joke that I was not sure he would understand in his young age. But after a few seconds, a smile broke out on his face as he said *"I get it! That's funny."* That is what eternal life will be like. In that day followers of Jesus will say *"Yes, this is exactly what it should be, more than I hoped for and better than I imagined. It is perfect, pleasing and good!"*

Keep this in mind, not one good thing of God will ever be lost for eternity. Followers of Jesus will not lose one good thing God planned for them. If something is good here on earth in the Lord, it is even better in eternity. For instance, consider the amazing variety of animals God created for this world. There are over 8.7 million species of plants and animals on this earth with 6.5 million species on land and 2.2 million in oceans Some wonder if there will be animals in God's eternal Kingdom? Of course! Why should we limit God's amazing creativity in heaven when He has so abundantly demonstrated it on earth? They will run, swim and fly throughout heaven. Why shouldn't they? God created them all in remarkable diversity, so why wouldn't He do so again with even greater multiplicity?

There are Bible verses that declare the presence of many animals in the new Kingdom of God. Isaiah 11:6-9 presents an extensive list of animals, some of which you may not expect to be there. (NIV) *"The wolf shall dwell with the lamb, and the leopard shall lie down with the young goat, and the calf and the lion and the fattened calf together; and a little child shall lead them. The cow and the bear shall graze; their young shall lie down together; and the lion shall eat straw like the ox. The nursing child shall play over the hole of the cobra, and the weaned child shall put his hand on the adder's den. They shall not hurt or destroy in all My holy mountain; for the earth shall be full of the knowledge of the LORD as the waters cover the sea."*

Wolfs, lambs, leopards, goats, lions, calves, cows, bears, cobras and adders live in harmony with babies and children in God's Kingdom. As all of them live fully embracing the knowledge of the Lord, not one of them hurts another. There, no destruction of life occurs, but an exuberance of enjoying life without fear or harm. Which of these images best convey to you the peace and joy found in the playfulness of humans and animals together? Would you like to lie down with a leopard or wander with a wolf? Would you like to leap with a lion or browse with a bear? Personally, I don't think I would enjoy playing with a cobra or adder snake, but I would love to spend time with bears. The point of these prophetic verses is to convey that everything of God's good creation continues in the next life, with greater good still to be discovered, as all will live in peace and harmony.

On a side note, let's review this often-asked question; "Will we have the same pets in heaven that we knew on this earth?" Because we invest so much emotion into our pets these days, some of you may not like the answer very much. Yes, there will be animals in the Lord's eternal kingdom including canines and felines. (We already read that in Isaiah above.) However, nowhere in the Bible does it state that a specific and singular animal that existed on this earth will be resurrected into the new Kingdom. One's particular pet named 'Fido', 'Rex', 'Fifi' or whatever may not be in heaven. Animals in this world do not have eternal souls. Only humans have eternal souls. We will have animals to enjoy in heaven, but there is no indication they will be exactly the same animal enjoyed as a pet on this earth. There will be dogs, cats and other animals, but maybe not your exact dog, cat or pet. However, the Lord can do anything, and this is not too great for Him to do, so, we will have to wait for the full answer to that question.

On the other hand, I have been asked if we will know specific individuals in that Kingdom such as our spouses, parents, children, good friends, etc.? The answer to that question is a resounding "Yes!" Humans do possess eternal souls. Eternal life begins with the Lord the moment anyone receives Him as their eternal Lord and Savior. So, those who live in Christ will know each other forever. That is why followers of Jesus should learn how to love and get along with each other now, because we are going to spend forever together. However, in Jesus' eternal Kingdom, relationships will be changed from the roles of spouses, children, parents, friends, etc. into a deeper dimension of family as brothers and sisters in the Lord Jesus. We won't relate to each other as we do now according to this earth's norms. Here we need mothers and fathers to care for children. There, all will experience the one True Father as His children and find themselves relating to each other as brothers and sisters in a way that is much greater than any brother or sister knows today.

This loss of our present familial relationships sounds like bad news to some. They might want to remain parent to their child, wife to a husband, or husband to a wife. This might be just a matter of losing control for some, which will be good for them to lose. In mature relationships, no one controls or dominates others. For example, it has been wonderful learning how to relate to my 3 grown children as adults rather than children. Most of the time, it is very enjoyable relating to 3 mature people who I dearly love and who love me in return, and of whom I no longer need to regulate their lives and activities. We are learning how to stand on an equal footing as caring adults for each other; the relationships we will enjoy forever.

Some fear a loss of intimacy and love in hearing this news. Jesus scares some of us when we read His words in Matthew 22:30 (NIV) *"For when the dead rise, they will neither marry nor be given in marriage. In this respect they will be like the angels in heaven."* Jesus did not give us any more information about this fact. The statement hangs there amidst a discussion in which He affirms the resurrection to eternal life with some who did not believe in that resurrection. But we don't have to feel threatened by Jesus' declaration about no marriage in heaven.

We know life will be infinitely more satisfying in the eternal Kingdom, and that includes our loving relationships. We can re-affirm our trust that God has this great promise in store for us.

Marriage in this life models a self-giving love in deeper relationships that all will experience and share forever in the eternal Kingdom. Marriage is not easy. We make vows to be faithful and strive to learn how to remain in a loving and uplifting relationship. Marriage prepares some of us to become ones who can love better for eternity. Marriage and parenting have done more for me than almost anything else to remove my selfishness and replace it with selflessness – the lifestyle of love for all in heaven.

Those who are single or childless learn this lesson in other ways. Too often single people or childless couples are made to feel inferior to married people, even in many churches. This is not true nor merited. Those who are single or childless in this life should in no way feel they will miss out on anything in heaven. In heaven, relationships will be of great selflessness toward others and inclusive of all, without the limitations we know on this earth. Here, our love is shallow and limited. There, our love will flow deeply without limit. As we discover that God is the deeper, unlimited Source of love for all His children and His family, there will be no constraints on sharing love together with Him and each other. The angels, as Jesus remarked, already know how to love in this way, and so will His people.

When people live together in eternal, all-good life with the Lord, the new dynamic of goodness and comprehensive love together fills their hearts and minds. Hebrews 8:10-12 (which is a re-sharing of Jeremiah 31:31-34) explains this important new dimension. (NIV) *"This is the covenant I will make with the house of Israel after that time, declares the Lord. I will put My laws in their minds and write them on their hearts. I will be their God, and they will be My people. No longer will a man teach his neighbor, or a man his brother, saying, 'Know the Lord,' because they will all know Me, from the least of them to the greatest. For I will forgive their wickedness and will remember their sins no more."*

What do you think it means to have God's laws placed in our minds and written on our hearts? That is an exciting, important and huge truth to understand. All of God's good life will flow through all of the lives and relationships in His eternal Kingdom. Biblically, hearts are the center of human nature and desires. Biblically, minds initiate human actions with thoughts. I understand this to mean that everyone by nature (who we are in our hearts) will desire only what God desires us to desire for good. And everyone in their thoughts (our minds) will think only what God designed us to think for good. Our hearts and minds will not conflict with each other as they so often do in this life. Here, my reason says *"No, don't do that because it is not good for you. Don't eat that extra cookie. Don't go spend that dollar on that unneeded knick-knack."* Meanwhile my desires tell me, *"But it tastes so good."* or *"It would be so fun to have!"* We know we should not take habit inducing drugs. Everyone knows that, but our desires have become enslaved to the rush of pleasure. We know we should not seek sexual release through pornography, but our twisted sexual desires have become so dominant. We give in to our desire and don't listen to our conscience. Now here is the good news: we won't face those conflicts between mind and heart, reason and desires in eternal life. Our hearts, minds, thoughts, desires, reasons and wants will all line up toward what is good, pleasing and perfect. God's eternal Law fulfilled in Jesus Christ will be lived out by each of us in the power and wisdom gained by our spirits living in harmony with God the Holy Spirit.

We will desire God's will for all of our lives to live in joyous conformity with it. Only those who conform themselves to seeking God's greater will can discover how good that is for them. As C. S. Lewis wrote *"There are only two kinds of people in the end: those who say to God, 'Thy will be done,' and those to whom God says, in the end, 'Thy will be done.' All that are in Hell, choose it. Without that self-choice, there could be no Hell. No soul that seriously and constantly desires joy will ever miss it. Those who seek find. Those who knock it is opened."* (**The Great Divorce**, pg. 90)

In heaven, everyone will know God and be led by Him. As we

heard in Isaiah, even the animals will be filled with His knowledge. (Which makes me wonder if they will be able to relate to us humans on a higher level there?) In the fullness of His knowledge flowing through us, we won't need anyone to instruct us on what is good. We will know it. (In this area, pastors will not be needed.) All will practice living goodness every moment together. As all wickedness will be removed and all forgiveness granted, we won't ever have to say we are sorry again, because we won't do anything that will need forgiveness. We won't want anything to do with wickedness again. We will live fully as God always intended for us to live in the abundance of His riches of goodness to us. This is eternal good life.

Please note that Hebrews 8:12 states that God *"...will remember sins no more."* That is great news for all of us and affects our eternal lives too. The memory of our past sins holds us back in this life. We retain a burden of guilt that grows every year from the many harms we inflict upon others. Things we did 20, 30, 40 years ago continue to haunt us. Even though we know Christ forgives us, we have a hard time letting go of our record of wrongs. In this world, past sins can come back with a vengeance. Things that occurred decades ago, as the headlines of today keep recording, topple politicians, celebrities, pastors, executives and many more. None of us is perfect, and we bear the shame of our past wrongs. These wrongs do need to be dealt with so that healing can occur for victims. However, I believe that people can change and learn from their errors. People don't need to be condemned forever.

When we confess our wrongs, seek forgiveness and find reconciliation, then we need to learn how to forgive and forget just as the Lord does for us. We need to let the Lord teach us how to deal with wrongs in appropriate ways and let them be forgotten. As much as we can, let us learn how to do that in this life. Let us not brand people as 'damned for eternity' or as 'hopeless wretches'. Let us learn to offer the healing grace of Jesus that we can forgive and reconcile through appropriate acts of restitution. Also, know that we will not carry these burdens of wrong into the new Kingdom of God. Since God will not remember our wrongs and banishes guilt from eternity, so we will not remember our wrongs. We will not be burdened by guilt and remorse. We will not bear grudges and ill will toward others. We will enjoy relationships without these detrimental feelings. We *"…will remember sins no more"* just as our Lord purposely does not remember our sins in loving grace for us.

It is so good to know that God's mercy through Jesus will set us free to live eternally together in all goodness. We don't deserve it, but Jesus shares loving grace with us anyway. As Mark Twain once remarked *"Heaven goes by favor. If it went by merit, you would stay out and your dog would go in."*

In the eternal good life with Jesus, we become more and more like Jesus in the goodness of His love, mercy and joy. As Jesus becomes the center of our lives: heart, body, mind and spirit, our lives reflect His goodness. The Apostle John declared this (John 17:3) (NIV) *"Now this is eternal life: that they may know You, the only true God, and Jesus Christ, whom You have sent."* The increase of our knowledge of Jesus in turn increases His good life among us. The great New England pastor and theologian Jonathan Edwards explained this. *"Therefore, their knowledge will increase to eternity; and if their knowledge, doubtless their holiness. For as they increase in the knowledge of God and of the works of God, the more they will see of his excellency; and the more they see of his excellency… the more will they love him; and the more they love God, the more delight and happiness… will they have in him."* (Edwards, The Miscellanies, The Works of Jonathan Edwards, Yale University Press, 1994, 275-76)

Let's end this chapter with these uplifting verses from Ephesians 1:3-10 (NIV) *"Praise be to the God and Father of our Lord Jesus Christ, who has blessed us in the heavenly realms with every spiritual blessing in Christ. For He chose us in Him before the creation of the world to be holy and blameless in His sight. In love He predestined us to be adopted as His sons through Jesus Christ, in accordance with His pleasure and will— to the praise of His glorious grace, which He has freely given us in the One He loves. In Him we have redemption through His blood, the forgiveness of sins, in accordance with the riches of God's grace that He lavished on us with all wisdom and understanding. And He made known to us the mystery of His will according to His good pleasure, which He purposed in Christ, to be put into effect when the times will have reached their fulfillment—to bring all things in heaven and on earth together under one head, even Christ."*

Our Lord Jesus Christ blessed us with every spiritual blessing in the heavenly realms. That is the eternal good Kingdom we look forward to with Him. Read again this list of blessings awaiting us:

- Chosen to be holy and blameless in His sight forever.
- Adopted as His children in Jesus Christ forever.
- Living in and by His pleasure and will forever.
- Living to the praise of His glorious grace forever.
- Living in the love of Jesus forever.
- Redeemed through His blood and forgiven forever.
- Revealing the mystery of His will according to His good pleasure in Christ forever.
- Living in great unity and harmony under the reign of Christ forever.
- All these blessings and many more await those who follow Jesus into His eternal good life.

ETERNAL LIFE RELATIONSHIPS

Life in God's Family

Key questions addressed in this chapter:
- Do those in heaven look down on the living in this life?
- What happens to people in the time between when they die and when they get into heaven?
- What will eternal relationships be like in heaven?

One of my favorite questions to ask people about eternal life is *"In addition to Jesus, who would you like to talk to in Heaven?"* My choices would be the prophet Elijah, King Saul's son Jonathan, the Apostle Paul, the great reformer Martin Luther, and my favorite author C. S. Lewis. Who would you like to meet? It will be fascinating to meet people from so many times, places and experiences who trust in the Lord. From what the Bible teaches, all will become fast friends; even more, the closest of brothers and sisters in His Heavenly family.

Have you ever met someone with whom you bonded immediately? I met Jim at the University of Colorado during our freshman year. We hit it off very well and became the closest of friends and brothers in Christ. After college, we did not see each other much, but kept in touch. We both got married and had children. After 15 years, we decided to get our families together on a vacation. We spent time together in the Colorado Rockies sharing a rental house and enjoyed a tremendous reunion. It was like the 15 years in between never existed. That example best describes for me eternal life relationships in the Kingdom of God where we will be united and enjoy a great reunion. Have you had a friend like my friend Jim? Sadly, Jim died from cancer a few years after that time. I so look forward to seeing him again in Christ's Kingdom. It will be like all the years in between without each other never existed.

Saying this, let's correct another misconception about eternal life. This misunderstanding gets repeated many times, often at memorial services. One of those sharing about their deceased loved one often will say that he knew this loved one is looking down at him in that moment. Others think their loved ones who have died are watching out for them too. We don't find these sentiments expressed anywhere in the Bible. And this will not be what any of us want to do when we enter the eternal Kingdom. We will not want to look back, but forward; unhindered with the cares of this world. We will be free from the concerns of this world with all its confusion and suffering, not looking down into it.

It is not that we won't care about those who live in this world. It is that we will be in a different dimension when it comes to time. For those who die in the Lord, this earth's time is gone the moment they enter into the eternal Kingdom. It is a little confusing, but the Bible teaches that one of 2 things happen to us when we die and prepare to enter into heaven. Some verses explain that, after death, most followers of Jesus enter into a kind of 'sleep' that will end on the Last Day when Christ returns to awaken them. 1 Corinthians 15:51-52 expresses this truth. (NIV) *"Listen, I tell you a mystery: We will not all sleep, but we will all be changed— in a flash, in the twinkling of an eye, at the last trumpet. For the trumpet will sound, the dead will be raised imperishable, and we will be changed."*

Paul infers that most will sleep until the last day, but some will not. Some of those who don't sleep will be those alive during the last days of this earth. They will be taken to meet Jesus directly. Others of those who don't sleep are the witnesses who confirm the judgment of evil. In Revelation 6:9, a special group of those who died as martyrs for Jesus call out for justice. It seems they have been roused from their sleep by the continued injustices raging upon the earth. They had suffered so much for the Lord and gave Him their all. They plead for the end of evil's tyranny by the righteous judgment of God. In this crucial moment of the end times, their plea is met with God's reassurance that all things will occur in the fullness of time. (This is the message any who have suffered unjustly need to hear from God. God is faithful and will bring vengeance against evil.) Then, they too are able to rest again, assured of God's faithfulness until the dawn of the New Kingdom of God. They will rise up to a great reward for their extraordinary witness to the Lord as they minister in the very throne room of God. (Revelation 7:14-17)

For all others, after death there is this 'sleeping.' Yet in that sleep it will seem that time does not exist. They wake up when Christ returns as if no time has passed. Have you ever been so tired that when your head rests on a pillow you fall into a deep sleep, then suddenly wake up with the sun shining in a new day? Hours have passed, but you never knew it. This will be the sleep of those who die in Christ. They lie down in death only to wake to the dawning of the new Day of Christ and wonder where the years went. It will be like the next day even though many days, years or centuries have passed. Paul seems to affirm this instantaneous sense of being with the Lord in Philippians 1:23 as He writes about His death. (NIV) *"I am torn between the two: I desire to depart and be with Christ, which is better by far;"* His departure from this world leads to his being with Christ. Death begins a jump which ends at eternal life with Christ. He reaffirms this again in 2 Corinthians 5:6-8 *"Therefore we are always confident and know that as long as we are at home in the body we are away from the Lord. For we live by faith, not by sight. We are confident, I say, and would prefer to be away from the body and at home with the Lord."* The hope and teaching of Paul is that death brings, not some living in limbo, purgatory, or wherever, waiting for the last day, but it actually brings one into being at home with the Lord for eternity.

We can only take so far certain alliterative devices used in the Bible, such as the parables of Jesus or the descriptions found in Revelation. They reveal key truths, but don't tell us everything. Jesus taught in parables to make a crucial point to those willing to hear. Parables are not allegories in which each thing represents a symbolic, hidden meaning. In the Parable of the Rich Man and Lazarus (Luke 16:19-31), Jesus intended to impress upon His hearers the necessity of hearing and obeying God's Law and, thus also, Jesus' teaching of the Word of God. Yet, it is fascinating to see that when lowly Lazarus dies, his soul seems immediately to enter into the presence of the greater life with God. In contrast, when the rich man dies, his soul seems immediately to enter into a place of torment – hell. Both seem instantaneous without being held in places of waiting for Judgment Day.

Jesus spoke of this quick passing through time when He told the thief on the cross next to His (who had affirmed his belief in Jesus - Luke 23:43). **(NIV)** *"Truly I tell you, today you will be with Me in paradise."* Loved ones who have passed away in the Lord are not looking down on us now. To us, still in this time, they sleep, yet they have awakened in their experience. They don't know the passing of time. They only know the *"today"* of Jesus and are with them. They pass beyond human time into the Day of the Lord. If you think logically about it, the rest of us, who also follow Jesus, will meet them on that same day too, just as they enter; ready to leave behind our past lives for the eternal good life that awaits. This life and its hard times will be gone, and kingdom life begins.

Allow me to say that this dimension of time passing in 'sleep' or what exactly happens for those awaiting the last days after death, is a great mystery. There is no way any of us who live in our present earthly second by second time frame can really grasp it. Others think differently on this than from what I have described. I share what I see is the Biblical answer and don't claim to be all knowing in this area. What we most certainly know and can fully agree upon is that there will come that day, whether it is long or short in coming, when we will be with the Lord to enter into His eternal Kingdom.

What will eternal life relationships be like for us? First and foremost, we will fully know Jesus and be fully known by Him. Earlier, we examined Jesus' words in John 17:3 (NIV) *"Now this is eternal life: that they may know You, the only true God, and Jesus Christ, whom You have sent."* In the Kingdom, we will fully know Jesus and God the Father. If you ask anyone who tries to love the Lord with all their heart, soul, mind and strength, their desire is to be with Jesus first and foremost. They would love to sit at His feet and listen to Him talk. They would be so honored to follow Him around and watch what He does. There is nothing better than to be with Jesus. Ask Mary, who sat at the feet of Jesus. Her sister Martha complained of this as she wanted Mary in the kitchen with her. But Jesus told Martha that Mary had chosen the better place of being with Him. In the eternal Kingdom, you won't need me or any pastor to tell you about Jesus' Word. You will know and hear from Him personally.

We will live with Jesus every day and live by the Holy Spirit all the time. He will live among us as our Light and Truth. He will be our Daily Bread of Life. He will be the First and the Last - the Alpha and Omega of our existence, our Resurrection Lord through death to eternity. We will see God face to face! Have you wondered what Jesus truly looks like? Many of the pictures of Jesus in our American and European churches are of Caucasian features. Jesus was not Caucasian. Other cultures portray Jesus as African, Eastern-Asian and Latin. He was not any of these. In His human life, He was of the Jewish race and would have looked much like them, Middle-Eastern in appearance. What will He look like for eternity? The great news is that we will find out. Revelation 22:3-4 promised (NIV) *"For the throne of God and of the Lamb will be there, and His servants will worship Him. And they will see His face, and His name will be written on their foreheads."*

Won't that be amazing to see Jesus and fully know Him! We will experience the fullness of His love, joy, grace and peace. We will watch His all mighty power control the universe. We will hear His omniscient wisdom in ruling over all peoples and creatures of His entire kingdom. Jesus will sit in the center of all at the right hand of God the Father Almighty, the hand of power and authority. And those who follow Jesus will witness it all in active praise and wonder. (If you want to get a glimpse of this heavenly worship, read Revelation Chapters 4 and 5.)

On the Day of Christ's return, when He ushers all of His followers into His eternal New Kingdom, we will run to Jesus. We will also run together in discovering the forever family in Christ. Some wonder what the phrase means that I include at the bottom of my emails – *"Further up and further in!"* This phrase comes from C. S. Lewis in an amazing land called Narnia. As illustrated in <u>The Chronicles of Narnia</u> books, Lewis filled Narnia with an amazing cast of very colorful and endearing characters. Every loyal creature citizen of Narnia humbly centered their relationships upon the Great Lion King Aslan. Indeed, the 7 books record the history of that land from its creation to its end. The final book, <u>The Last Battle,</u> narrates the day of Aslan's final return to Narnia and the beginning of a new and greater Narnia. After the demise of the first Narnia and all its world, every one of those colorful Narnian characters, whom you come to love so much in reading about them, find themselves running together up the hills toward the center of a new Narnia; a more beautiful and richer Narnia. If you have read the books, you will know these characters: Peter, Lucy, Edmond, King Caspian, Eustace, the Unicorn Jewel, Puddleglum the Marshwiggle, Reepicheep the Noble Mouse, King Tirian, and many more race further up and further in to meet Aslan in His New Kingdom. Here is the explanation of this in the words of Jewel the Unicorn. *"It was the Unicorn who summed up what everyone was feeling. He stamped his right fore-hoof on the ground and neighed and then cried: 'I have come home at last! This is my real country! I belong here. This is the land I have been looking for all my life, though I never knew it till now. The reason why we loved the old Narnia is that it's sometimes looked a little like this. Come further up, come further in!"* (C. S. Lewis, <u>The Last Battle</u>, pg. 171)

The future in eternity will be like this for the followers of Jesus.

In His New Kingdom; Adam and Eve, Abraham and Sarah, Isaac, Rebekah, Jacob/Israel, Joseph, Moses and Miriam, Joshua, Gideon, Sampson, Samuel, Ruth and Boaz, King David, Jonathan, Hezekiah, Jeremiah, Esther, Danial, Peter, John, James, Paul, Barnabas, and so many more beloved people of the Bible will congregate around the Lord's throne. So also will Augustine, Thomas Aquinas, Martin Luther, John Calvin, John Wesley, Jonathan Edwards, C. S. Lewis, John Stott, and many more of the noted followers of Jesus gather there. Yet the Kingdom will not be populated by just the famous. Men and women from all times, places and ethnicities who faithfully followed Jesus in obscure situations will gather there around Him too. People like you and me, but also not like us at all. All will be gathered because of the One True Savior and Lord. Won't that be amazing to be there with them all!

We will live in the family of God with all followers of Jesus as brothers and sisters. We hear of this prolific and diverse gathering of people in Ephesians 2:19. (NIV) *"Consequently, you are no longer foreigners and aliens, but fellow citizens with God's people and members of God's household..."* No foreigners and aliens live in the Kingdom, but fellow members of God's household. There are no second or lower-class citizens there. Everyone will have the full rights of free citizens of that kingdom. Everyone will have complete access to God the Father, Son and Holy Spirit. Everyone will enjoy all the benefits of their citizenship and will be joint heirs as family members. Unlimited resources of rich life flow from the Father to His eternal sons and daughters. While our unique makeup will continue in character traits and distinctiveness, with all the good aspects of our heritage and race remaining, none of those things will divide or cause harm. All people and things will come together with their rich diversity into a greater harmony of life together in Christ.

All are sons of God as it refers to our inheritance of God the Father's riches. This erases what used to be the distinctions that divide in this earth: rich or poor, Jew or Gentile, male or female.

Now there are no longer barriers of any kind between humans. The Apostle Paul described this inheritance in Galatians 3:26-29. (NIV) *"You are all sons of God through faith in Christ Jesus, for all of you who were baptized into Christ have clothed yourselves with Christ. There is neither Jew nor Greek, slave nor free, male (and) female, for you are all one in Christ Jesus. If you belong to Christ, then you are Abraham's seed, and heirs according to the promise."*

We don't become autonomously the same in eternal life. We remain unique in our personality, good characteristics and heritage. Yet, as some of these traits remain in our eternal makeup, they cause no divisions in God's Kingdom because of our race, ethnicity, language, economy or gender. All are joint heirs with Christ in God's family; meaning all receive and enjoy the same blessings and benefits of that status. This eternal promise should help us in our present relationships to learn how to break down any human divisions that come between us. United in Christ by the Holy Spirit we can practice in any church family how to let our past diversity help us enjoy greater harmony.

Pastor Keith Fink of the Great Valley Presbyterian Church of Malvern, PA shared about this vital lesson for us. *"If we are citizens of heaven - then the church should be an outpost of that 'country' in this fallen world - an embassy if you will - representing to the world our true home - our life together should offer glimpses, hints, imperfect tastes, of the kingdom to which we belong. And certainly, those hints should be seen most clearly in how we do life together - that should seem counter-cultural to the non-believing world - they ought to say to one another 'see how they love one another.'"*

We have so much to look forward to in the eternal Kingdom of the Lord. Keep looking through the Bible to find more truths and hints of what it will be like. And realize again, that the more we open our relationships to the living Lord among us, the more we grow in our eternal relationships today. And then one day, we can shout together *"Further up and further in!"*

ETERNAL LIFE BODIES

The Fullness of Life

Key questions addressed in this chapter:
- Will people become ghostly spirits floating about in space or will they have bodies of real flesh and bones?
- What age will people be in the kingdom of heaven?
- Will people fly around with wings or will they still have human limitations keeping them on the ground?
- Will people of heaven be able to eat and drink?

(Keep in mind as we address these questions that the Bible does not explain everything, just some of the basics. Many wonderful surprises await those who will inhabit the eternal Kingdom.)

What will bodies be like in heaven? We find a snapshot of heavenly bodies in Philippians 3:20-21. (NIV) *"But our citizenship is in heaven. And we eagerly await a Savior from there, the Lord Jesus Christ, who, by the power that enables Him to bring everything under His control, will transform our lowly bodies so that they will be like His glorious body."* A snapshot gives a quick first impression. This snapshot of heavenly bodies reveals a heavenly body like Jesus. I shared before about the transformation that occurs for followers of Jesus when He takes them into His eternal Kingdom. The Bible term for this is 'glorification.' In this glorification, the Lord purifies the hearts and minds of His followers so that every thought, desire, and action will only be good and right all the time. Not a single evil thought will be in any mind, nor will any harmful, corrupted desire in any heart exist in that kingdom. All will be good, as nothing will mar the perfection of morality and healthy relationships. These verses share about this transformative power of Jesus to bring everything under His control so that all will live in His good, pleasing and perfect will. Notice that the second half of verse 21 expands this transformation to include the body also.

Michael Paul Clark

All followers of Jesus will enjoy transformed thoughts, desires and bodies - glorious ones like His.

What do you think it means to have a glorious body like Jesus? Our imaginations dream up unlimited possibilities for this wondrous body. However, we should constrain our imaginings to only the human side of Jesus, not the divine side. Jesus was, is and always will be fully God. There is only One God known to us in the Trinity of God the Father, Son and Holy Spirit. Followers of Jesus do not become gods in eternity. In the miracle of His birth, Jesus revealed the fullness of God as well as the fullness of humanity to humans. It is in this second side of His revelation – to be fully human - that the followers of Jesus become like Him. To be fully human means living without any wrong or corruption; the perfect humanity as God the Father originally intended. In this transformation, His followers become fully human as Jesus was in His incarnation (God in the flesh) and is for eternity. The first humans lost this opportunity to learn what it meant to be fully human as God created them when they disobeyed God. Followers of Jesus regain this humanity, without the consequences of the Fall. In the eternal Kingdom of God, followers of Jesus have the fullness of life in the abundance of only good all the time.

These few verses in Philippians don't tell us anything more about this new glorious body. However, the Apostle Paul shared more details in 1 Corinthians 15:42-52. As it is a long passage, let's take it in sections. (NIV) "*So will it be with the resurrection of the dead. The body that is sown is perishable, it is raised imperishable; it is sown in dishonor, it is raised in glory; it is sown in weakness, it is raised in power; it is sown a natural body, it is raised a spiritual body. If there is a natural body, there is also a spiritual body.*"

Renewed human glorious bodies are not perishable. They are imperishable. When God created humans, He created them for eternal life not death. Death resulted from turning away from God the Source of Life. However, in Christ His followers become eternal people again - in spirit only in this world, but in both spirit and body in His eternal Kingdom. The word '*imperishable*' in regard to bodies reveals that decay or death in any form no longer exist. Kingdom bodies don't age. They don't lose their teeth, hair or muscle tone. They don't have more aches with each passing year. They become eternally imperishable.

What will these bodies look like in terms of youthful looks? Many ponder what age they will be in heaven? Recently after the death of President George H. W Bush, many commentators shared about his life. One of the sad times of his life was when he and his wife Barbara lost a 3-year-old daughter. It was shared that President Bush wondered, when he met his daughter in heaven, what age she would be? Would she still be 3 years old or would she be older? I heard a pastor at a memorial service proclaim that in eternity everyone will look 18 years of age or so. He felt that was the best age to be physically; full of vigor yet also with maturity. So, in his opinion that was the age all would be in heaven. This is a common question that many ask.

The Bible answers this question differently from what many expect. An age in this life, such as 3, 18, 29, 45, 66 or 92 is an earthly age number that shows a present-day human perspective. Human bodies shine with youth and vigor in early years then wane and wither in older years. 18 years to humans conveys youth and vigor while 88 conveys increasing weakness and ailments. With ageless bodies, you don't look 3, 18, 50, or 90 as you would have on earth; you look as God intends you to appear for eternity, fully mature yet eternally youthful. Heavenly bodies are ageless bodies, not bound by specific years. They don't lose energy, vitality, beauty, or tone each year. Pain does not increase as it does not exist. Aching joints or loss of hair will not be a problem. The eternal body remains the same in strength, looks and wisdom at age 29, 129, 1299, and for eternity.

I believe that those in eternity will have a youthfulness that makes us think they are quite young, yet also a wisdom that makes us think they are very old. The benefits of both youth and experience manifest together in a timeless, imperishable body. I met a friend from High School whom I had not seen in 40 years. I instantly recognized him, and he also recognized me. Yes, we looked older, but we still retained that inherent personhood that came in our birth. The inner soul shone through to the eyes of a long-term friend. In heaven, bodies don't age. They do reflect the wholeness of a person: body, spirit, and mind. The combined essence of these three parts of our being is greater than the sum of the individual parts. Each of us is not just what we look like to others physically. In heaven, each part of our being unite in a marvelous integrity that radiates. A fullness of life comes from a completely healthy body, a totally sound mind, and an eternal, empowering spirit. So, we will not look like we are 10, 30 or 70 years of age. We will look ageless, wise and loving.

Renewed human glorious bodies have power not weakness. They don't fatigue or fail. They don't run down or break down. They keep going with strength and vigor. They remain constantly able to perform up to full potential. Heavenly human glorious bodies power by the spirit, not by natural resources. Natural bodies in this world gain power through harnessing energy from food sources. They need constant material sustenance, or they grow weary, losing energy. Spiritual bodies find their source of energy through their renewed spiritual linkage to God the Holy Spirit. Physical bodies unite with the spiritual dimension that was lost in the Fall of humanity. They reengage with the Holy Spirit. Energy flows from the Holy Spirit through the human spirit to the body of the kingdom person. It is a whole new source of energy, much like solar energy provides power for homes instead of the energy of electricity that comes from limited natural resources like coal or oil. Spiritual energy cannot be exhausted as it comes from the unlimited power and life source of God the Holy Spirit. (Followers of Jesus discover some of this spiritual energy in this world when they use the spiritual gifts given by the Holy Spirit for ministry.)

Heavenly human bodies are glorious in perfection not dishonored and corrupted by sin. This is the glorified body that comes through Jesus as the Son of Man, the Second Adam, or as the Apostle Paul calls Him - the Man from heaven. 1 Corinthians 15:45-49 (NIV) *"So it is written: 'The first man Adam became a living being'; the last Adam, a life-giving spirit. The spiritual did not come first, but the natural, and after that the spiritual. The first man was of the dust of the earth, the second Man from heaven. As was the earthly man, so are those who are of the earth; and as is the Man from heaven, so also are those who are of heaven. And just as we have borne the likeness of the earthly man, so shall we bear the likeness of the Man from heaven."*

God created Adam from the earth and breathed a spirit into him. He was flesh and spirit. This spirit dimension separated Adam from all the other animals who were only of the physical earth. Eve came from Adam's side in the Lord's power and she too became flesh and spirit. This spiritual dimension of connection to the Holy Spirit died for both of them in the Fall of humanity. Humans lost the spiritual relationship to God the Source of life. So, from dust they came and to dust they returned. They began to decay and then died in physical form when they lost the Source of life.

This was never God's intention or design. Humans were not created to die. That is why we grieve so much the loss of loved ones. However, in His gracious plan of salvation, God sent Jesus to remedy this loss and restore us to Him eternally. He came as the Son of God to fully reveal God to humanity. And as was noted, He also came as the Son of Man to fully reveal true humanity to fallen humans and restore them. When we want to know what real humanity is like, we look to Jesus. It is this dimension of Jesus' humanity Paul wrote about in this passage. The second Man from heaven brings back the spiritual dimension, the spiritual relationship to God the Source of Life. He restores the true humanity as the last Adam (because we will never need another) who brings healing (resurrection) for the wrongs of the first Adam. In this healing of restoration and transformation Jesus rebirths in humanity the life-giving spirit from God. ("*Born from above*" as Jesus shared with Nicodemus in John 3) Thus, all those of heaven are like the glorified Son of Man, the last Adam who restored humanity through His resurrection.

Paul then clarified how and when this glorification happens in 1 Corinthians 15:50-52. (NIV) "*I declare to you, brothers and sisters, that flesh and blood cannot inherit the Kingdom of God, nor does the perishable inherit the imperishable. Listen, I tell you a mystery: We will not all sleep, but we will all be changed— in a flash, in the twinkling of an eye, at the last trumpet. For the trumpet will sound, the dead will be raised imperishable, and we will be changed.*"

Note carefully that eternal Kingdom people do not gain some new body that is totally unrelated to what their human bodies were like in appearance in this earth. The present body is raised and transformed when Jesus returns, yet it retains its inherent, created, unique identity. This includes all bodies lost due to the ravages of time, catastrophe and decay. This includes bodies buried, lost at sea, or cremated. God brings restoration with reconciliation. Jesus is the Resurrection and the Life. Whatever happened to the first bodies His followers lived in in this current world does not deny them the new heavenly body. What God intended each one to look like in human form will be recreated so that each person is recognizable and appreciated in God's image - in each one's renewed beautiful distinctiveness.

Some wonder if there is eating and drinking with the new resurrection bodies? A misunderstanding of 1 Corinthians 6:13 might make us think they won't happen. It reads (NIV) "*You say, 'Food for the stomach and the stomach for food, and God will destroy them both.'*" Reading just this phrase out of context makes us think that after death we won't have stomachs or food, but that is not what this verse taught. The context of this passage is one of speaking about earthly desires that cause problems. This is what God destroys. Once this life is over on this earth, when this earthly body dies, all such confused desires will also die. But in the future Kingdom life, not only will eating happen in the eternal Kingdom, it will occur in balance and enjoyment. (No need for diets.) Jesus shared that He will eat and drink with His disciples in the Kingdom of God in Luke 22:14-18,29-30. (NIV) "*When the hour came, Jesus and His apostles reclined at the table. And He said to them, 'I have eagerly desired to eat this Passover with you before I suffer. For I tell you, I will not eat it again until it finds fulfillment in the kingdom of God.' After taking the cup, He gave thanks and said, 'Take this and divide it among you. For I tell you I will not drink again of the fruit of the vine until the kingdom of God comes. And I confer on you a kingdom, just as My Father conferred one on Me, so that you may eat and drink at My table in My kingdom and sit on thrones, judging the twelve tribes of Israel.'*" Jesus will eat and drink with His people. Communion celebrations in the church, when gathered in Jesus' name, look forward to this gathering around the Lord's Table in the eternal Kingdom, eating and drinking with Jesus as He promised.

Jesus' appearances after His resurrection reveal more about the future, glorious human body. There were several of these appearances. One occurs in Luke 24:36-43 (NIV) "*While they were still talking about this, Jesus himself stood among them and said to them, 'Peace be with you.' They were startled and frightened, thinking they saw a ghost. He said to them, 'Why are you troubled, and why do doubts rise in your minds? Look at My hands and My feet. It is I myself! Touch Me and see; a ghost does not have flesh and bones, as you see I have.' When He had said this, He showed them His hands and feet. And while they still did not believe it because of joy and amazement, He asked them, 'Do you have anything here to eat?' They gave Him a piece of broiled fish, and He took it and ate it in their presence.*"

Jesus has a real and solid resurrection body with flesh and bones. He can be recognized and touched. He can eat. As this is true for Jesus in His transformed resurrection body, it will be true for the fully human, transformed, resurrection body. Yet, notice that Jesus in this glorified state transcends the limitations of the present human body. He appears among them, seeming to pass through the solid walls. The disciples thought He was a ghost because of this. However, just the opposite actually occurred. Jesus had the real, greater body. The disciple's human bodies and, indeed, the walls of their room were the more ghostly, lesser realities to Jesus. The new spiritual, physical body enjoys the greater reality.

This happens again in another resurrection appearance by Jesus in John 20:19-20. (NIV) *"On the evening of that first day of the week, when the disciples were together, with the doors locked for fear of the Jewish leaders, Jesus came and stood among them and said, 'Peace be with you!' After He said this, He showed them His hands and side. The disciples were overjoyed when they saw the Lord."* Jesus stands among them as the locked doors cannot stop Him. He showed them again His hands and side to get them to see He is real and not a ghost. How can this be? It can only be because Jesus is greater in body and spirit. The walls and doors of this world are like vapors to Him in His greater reality. Jesus appeared several times to spend time with His disciples before He ascended to heaven. He ate with His disciples at least 2 other times; appearing along the Sea of Galilee eating fish and on the Road to Emmaus eating bread. Each time Jesus demonstrated the reality of His physical, spiritual body that transcended human experiences of this earth's dimensions.

If you would like to get a better understanding of this concept of a greater physical reality in God's Kingdom with the physical presence in this world as the ghostly existence, I encourage you to read an allegory of this as found in C. S. Lewis' book <u>The Great Divorce</u>. A human from this world takes a bus trip to the Kingdom of God. When He gets there, everything is greater. His eyes have to get used to the greater light because all previous light was much less bright. His feet must get used to the greater solid of the ground. Even the grass he walks on there hurts his feet because his feet are too soft and the grass too solid for them. The citizens of that kingdom who meet them walk and run with ease and without pain, while the ghostly earth travelers struggle to keep up. It is a fun read and gives a glimpse of the possible greater reality of glorious bodies for the future eternal Kingdom.

Jesus' resurrected body, although glorified and eternal, did show the scars of His crucifixion and death. Will heavenly bodies of those who enter heaven retain their scars also? Jesus' scars represent the great love He demonstrated through the trials and tortures of His death. They symbolize His work of saving humanity in His mercy and grace. In His appearance before Thomas, those scars reveal to Thomas that his loving Lord actually stands before him. Jesus still loves Thomas even though Thomas doubted Him. The scars help Peter to remove His doubts. Those scars help us to remove all doubts too of how much Jesus loves us. He loves us eternally through giving His life for our life, taking our consequences for our wrongs upon Himself. When all see Jesus and His scars face to face, they bow down in awe and wonder for His sacrificial love. Thus, Jesus' scars are important marks of Jesus' love. The citizens of heaven however will have no use for scars. Their bodies will be completely healed of all memories of past suffering. They will enjoy fresh, renewed heavenly bodies.

One more key Bible verse also hints at the greater possibilities that followers of Jesus experience in the eternal Kingdom of God. Isaiah 40:31 shares about life in that place. (NIV) *"But those who trust in the LORD will find new strength. They will soar high on wings like eagles. They will run and not grow weary. They will walk and not faint."* Kingdom people will not grow weary but can run all day. They can walk without fatigue. And, maybe, there will be wings in heaven because kingdom people will soar like eagles. We don't know how much eternal Kingdom bodies will be capable of doing, but we do know it will be exciting, wonderful and glorious enjoying abundant life forever in them.

ETERNAL LIFE PURPOSE

The Meaning of Eternal Life

Key questions addressed in this chapter:
- What will make life purposeful, meaningful and enjoyable forever?
- What will worship be like in Heaven?
- Will people know everything in heaven and be perfect in every way?

What gives life purpose? What makes life meaningful? These questions are very important for finding joy in this life. These same questions become vitally important when you ask them about eternal life. We can enjoy, and if need be, endure some things for a short time, but what about for eternity? Think how dreadful life will be if what we do for eternity is drab and inconsequential. What will make life purposeful, meaningful and enjoyable forever? In this examination of eternal life, once again the Bible has the answers to our questions.

There are four purposes of life to provide meaning and joy every day and forever. These four purposes bring greater life today and abundant life forever. They are: 1) Worship: to glorify and enjoy God forever. 2) Fellowship: to love and enjoy each other forever. 3) Ministry: to encourage and serve each other forever. 4) Discipleship: to keep growing in Christ in knowledge, wisdom and ability forever. Let's examine each one. (The 5th great purpose for life on this earth is evangelism – sharing the Good News about Jesus that leads them to Him. In God's eternal Kingdom, all will know the Lord, so this is the only purpose that is not eternal.)

1) Worship: To Glorify and Enjoy God Forever.

Revelation chapters 4 & 5 portray the dramatic pageant of eternal worship. God sits on His brilliant and indescribable throne ringed by an aura of majestic colors in brilliant glory. Around His throne fly incredible creatures whose sole purpose is to wait upon His every command. Circles of angels and elders radiate out from His throne alternately praising God in worship and awe. Such a sight exceedingly surpasses the grandest of human coronations, inaugurations, galas, festivities or gatherings of any kind. The worship continues with choreographed precision and euphoric outbursts of honor to the only One worthy of such acclamation. If you can imagine yourself among those who join in this worship (because in the presence of the Almighty God, no one passively watches, but instinctively participates), it will be the grandest experience of eternal life.

As the worship continues, the Lion of Judah enters as the Lamb of God who overcomes all wrongs, evil and death. The Lamb Who is the Christ, is the only one able and prepared to carry out God's plan to redeem His people and bring them into His eternal Kingdom. We pick up the description in Revelation 5:11-14 (NIV) *"Then I looked and heard the voice of many angels, numbering thousands upon thousands, and ten thousand times ten thousand. They encircled the throne and the living creatures and the elders. In a loud voice they were saying: 'Worthy is the Lamb, who was slain, to receive power and wealth and wisdom and strength and honor and glory and praise' Then I heard every creature in heaven and on earth and under the earth and on the sea, and all that is in them, saying: 'To Him who sits on the throne and to the Lamb be praise and honor and glory and power, for ever and ever!' The four living creatures said, 'Amen,' and the elders fell down and worshiped."* Do you see yourself there in that amazing worship of Jesus? Every creature of heaven, earth, sea and under the earth join to praise God. If you are a true follower of Jesus, you will be there in that universal worship service to glorify God.

Worship of God undergirds all the activities of God's people in the eternal Kingdom. That worship includes both praise and behaviors that honor God every moment. Worship is and will be continuous in every word and deed of God's people. The words for 'worship' in both the Old Testament Hebrew and the New Testament Greek mean both to work and to worship in honor of God. Often that eternal worship occurs simultaneously in such grand gatherings. Other times it happens wherever God's people meet together to bring Him glory. In this worship, God is there among them. Every work of their hands and ever word of their mouths add to this honoring worship of God. When they build or create something, it will be in glory to God. When they play or feast together, it will reflect His loving nature. When they gather, they always gather in His name with the Lord Jesus among them. We can learn a lot from this eternal worship about worship here and now. We learn to let every word that comes from our mouths be edifying and uplifting in such a way that we would not be embarrassed to say it in the presence of the Lord. We learn to let every behavior that comes from our hearts and minds be encouraging and caring as a witness to the One who loves us so much that He died for us.

I don't have trouble with those who say they worship at the beach, in the mountains or anywhere in the grandeur of nature. Nature reveals the glory of God. What I object to is when they say those places take precedence over worship with the family of God. Worship with God's family is greater. God is all about reconciling and enjoying relationships. Worship unites us as we praise God. Worship centers us together in the Holy Spirit. Worship lifts us into the presence of the Lord. Jesus gives special reward to those who gather in His name by promising that He is among them. All worship in word and deed centered on the Lord will bring great joy and meaning every day in the eternal Kingdom. C. S. Lewis describes this joyful worship, *"The Scotch catechism says that man's chief end is 'to glorify God and enjoy Him forever.' But we shall then know that these are the same thing. Fully to enjoy is to glorify. In commanding us to glorify Him, God is inviting us to enjoy Him."* (Reflections on the Psalms, pg. 96) Therefore, the first great purpose of eternal life is to worship God.

2) Fellowship: To Love and Enjoy Each Other Forever.

A second great purpose to eternal life will be enjoying deep and intimate relationships with the sisters and brothers of God's eternal family. The Apostle Paul explained the deep bonds shared in that eternal family in Ephesians 2:19 (NLT) *"So now you Gentiles are no longer strangers and foreigners. You are citizens along with all of God's holy people. You are members of God's family."* In God's family, no one is a stranger, alien, foreigner or outcast. No one who belongs in the eternal family of God will ever feel any sense of loneliness. All will enjoy every benefit, right and freedom as citizens of His eternal Kingdom. Every person in that healthiest of families (for there, no dysfunctional family exists), enjoys the company of each other.

The name of God's true family is the universal Church (with a capital C to separate it from the local church). In this true gathering in Christ, all exist for each other in unified love. All are lifted up. All find any help they can use. All are selfless as they live for each other. Pastor Rick Warren described the Church in this way *"The church is God's agenda for the world. Jesus said, 'I will build my church, and all the powers of hell will not conquer it.' The church is indestructible and will exist for eternity. It will outlive this universe, and so will your role in it."* (The Purpose Driven Life: What on Earth Am I Here For? p. 168. Zondervan. Kindle Edition.)

Think of all the adventures to be enjoyed together in the eternal Kingdom. A whole new world will be ready to explore; a world without terrors or troubles, with amazing diversity of nature and gorgeous panoramas of scenery. (More about this in a few chapters.) Life is meant to be shared. We love to celebrate accomplishments with close family and friends. We feast together as we laugh and tell embellished tales of past joyful experiences. Family feasts and friendship celebrations give a glimpse of the eternal family celebrations to come, especially the ones gathered at Christ's Feast Table. Real fellowship is authentic, not superficial with false fronts. With people you can trust and love, whom you also know will trust and love you, you genuinely and openly share of yourselves together. Here on earth, we look for those who like us in spite of our faults. They are true friends. In the eternal Kingdom, where we will have no faults (yet still individual distinctive traits), we will enjoy the true and genuine love of all the sisters and brothers in Christ. I will write more about this in next chapter as I describe these eternal relationships. This is enough description here to show that the 2nd great purpose in eternal life is loving and enjoying each other forever.

3) Ministry: To Encourage and Serve Each Other Forever.

This one might surprise you, but the 3rd great purpose for eternal life will be to minister to God and to each other - to encourage and serve each other forever. Some might think that any ministry will not be needed in heaven, but some ministry will be very beneficial indeed. Revelation 22:1-5 shares the perspective on this ministry. (NIV) *"Then the angel showed me the river of the water of life, as clear as crystal, flowing from the throne of God and of the Lamb down the middle of the great street of the city. On each side of the river stood the tree of life, bearing twelve crops of fruit, yielding its fruit every month. And the leaves of the tree are for the healing of the nations. No longer will there be any curse. The throne of God and of the Lamb will be in the city, and His servants will serve Him. They will see His face, and His name will be on their foreheads. There will be no more night. They will not need the light of a lamp or the light of the sun, for the Lord God will give them light. And they will reign for ever and ever."*

In the Garden of Eden stood two majestic trees surrounded by many other beautiful trees. One was the tragic Tree of the Knowledge of Good and Evil; from which the first couple ate and disobeyed God. The other was the Tree of Life; from which God banished the humans so they would not live in their corruption and evil forever. In the new Garden of Eden, the new paradise of the eternal Kingdom, God lives again among His people. Eternal life flows like a river from His throne as He is the Source of Life. On each side of this river stand not one but two Trees of Life to signify the greater life available to those who follow Christ into His eternal Kingdom. Then, instead of being barred from eating of the Tree of Life, all can return to the Tree and take of its leaves and fruit for healing from the travails and trials of the past life on earth. All of this symbolizes the restorative cure for mind, body and soul that Jesus shares from God the Father to His people.

Even as God continues to serve His people, His love flows back to Him in the ministry of His people. They desire to serve Him in gratitude for all that He has done for them. Verse 3 said that *"His servants will serve Him."* How will they serve Him? How do you serve a God who has no needs? By offering up not only their words of worship, but also by offering up their acts of service to God's people. Like the priests and Levites who served in God's earthly temple, some of them will help lead in the gatherings of worship and celebration of God. They will lead the people in songs, thanksgivings, and various other acts of worship. The Lord has always commended and thanked His followers for helping others in His name. As He mentioned in Matthew 25:40 (NIV) *"Truly I tell you, whatever you did for one of the least of these brothers and sisters of Mine, you did for Me."*

Remember that in the Old Testament times, the Temple was the place to bring sacrifices. Most of those sacrifices were for the sins and wrongs the people committed against God and others. They brought animals to be slaughtered on the altar, so the blood of the innocent animals would seek to atone for the forgiveness of the erring people. Jesus, once and for all time, became the ultimate sacrificial Lamb Who took away all penalties for wrong and sin. The people of God no longer need to make any bloody, sin offerings from the time of Jesus' cross. However, in the Old Testament there were other types of offerings. They were offerings of praise and thanksgiving for the generosity (blessings) of God. These offerings continue today and will continue for eternity. People from all over the Kingdom of God will gather to offer their sacrifice of praise and thanksgiving. They will serve the Lord where they live and in the Holy City of the New Jerusalem. They will offer their service to each other in the name of the Lord. This is the reason why God's people wear His name. They are His and they serve in His name. They have seen God and, like Moses, His radiant being enlightens them with His glory.

The people will use the gifts of the Holy Spirit they have been given to make God's Kingdom a wonderful place full of joy and creativity. As no one will be in need, some gifts will change their purpose. Some will not be needed at all such as the gifts of evangelism or mercy, but most will continue. Some will serve God and each other with ready hands in the gift of helping. Some will lead worship in the gifts of prayer, exhortation and music. Some will build wonderful structures and create beautiful art with the gifts of craftsmanship and skills. Some will teach one another of God's truth. Some will proclaim the goodness of God in their athletic, intellectual and creative prowess in glorious competitions (a heavenly Olympics). Some will use gifts of leadership and administration to create exhilarating events for all to enjoy (concerts, plays, great entertainment). Others will mentor and coach others in mastering many different skills and endeavors. All the good talents, abilities and gifts God granted to His people to help each other enjoy life will remain and mature to use for eternity. In serving each other, they serve God. Eternal life in God's eternal Kingdom will be the opposite of boring. The creativity, imagination, gifts, skills, talents and all the marvelous abilities of God's people will be set free to soar in their serving and ministry to help each other enjoy life eternal every day.

4) Discipleship: To Keep on Growing in Christ in Knowledge, Wisdom and Ability Forever.

The fourth purpose that brings meaning and fulfillment for eternity is maturing forever as disciples of Jesus Christ. There will be countless opportunities to grow in knowledge, wisdom and abilities. The infinite God keeps many surprises waiting for His followers. The unending store of God's good treasures and riches become available for His people to discover and experience. The Apostle James speaks about the riches available for God's people to discover. James 1:17-18 (NLT) *"Whatever is good and perfect is a gift coming down to us from God our Father, who created all the lights in the heavens. He never changes or casts a shifting shadow. He chose to give birth to us by giving us His true Word. And we, out of all creation, became His prized possession."*

We cannot list all the good and perfect gifts that God showers upon His people. God is the greatest of all givers. God invented giving. God loves to generously share His gifts with His people. Why? Because, as James shared, His people are His prize possessions. In other words, His people are the ones He values and loves the most. God is not into material things. He can create all sorts of things in abundance at any time; including what we think of as rare or valuable things such as gems or gold. Those are so abundant in God's eternal Kingdom that they are common building materials. God values His people. God never held back His greatest gift of His Son for His people. He won't hold back all the treasures of Heaven for His people to enjoy.

Everything God created is good and will be in the eternal Kingdom in a new and unspoiled way. Even more mysteries of God await His people to explore and experience for joy and enlightenment. God will give free reign to our human curiosity to investigate the universe. We will have time abundant to improve our skills and talents. In the classic movie "Groundhog Day", one man keeps living the same day over and over. After he tires of this same day lived many times over the same way, he tries to live in other ways that he thinks will pleasure his selfish desires. Eventually finding this selfishness empty, he becomes depressed and invents new ways to kill himself, but he still wakes up again to the same day. Eventually he decides to better himself. He learns to play the piano with finesse and flair. He seeks out ways to help people and finds great reward in that. He stops being selfish in learning to be selfless. Of course, this makes him more attractive to the woman he really likes, who detested his selfish old self. Eventually, she cannot help but like this new man. In eternal life, a new every day presents boundless opportunity to better minds, character, serving, talents and skills. We will become better and better with no end to the growth we can experience. I look forward to this time of amazing life, researching and inventing new ways of enjoying it together.

This reminds me of what happens when an infant becomes a toddler. So much phenomenal growth and maturity happens in such a short time. The infant learns to crawl then walk then run. The toddler learns to utter words then talk then communicate. Their mind and bodies develop at an astounding pace. Such will be the development of the new children of God the Father. Released from the enslavements and limitations of this corrupted world, their imaginations and creativity coupled with their unbounded spirit and energy, grow increasingly. This discovery of God's truth for greater living together with Him and each other produces a growth in maturity greater than we have ever known, that keeps compounding every new day.

God's Kingdom will not be boring. Life there will be eternally fulfilling in meaning and purpose as we worship in glory, fellowship in love, serve in joy, and grow in exciting discipleship with Jesus and each other. However, though much of this waits for us in that eternal Kingdom, some of it is already available to us now if we will open our hearts and minds even more to the leading of God the Holy Spirit with us. We can enjoy far more of this life than perhaps we thought we could, and then have so much more to look forward to with the Lord forever.

ETERNAL LIFESTYLE

Always Speaking and Living the Truth in Love

Key questions addressed in this chapter:
- Will doing good things in heaven be enjoyable and pleasing?
- What are the lifestyles like of those who reside in heaven?
- Will people still have the fruit of the Holy Spirit in heaven?

In our exploration of eternal life as the Bible explains it, we have discovered: the perfect timing, total lack of evil, complete good and deep relationships, amazing bodies and purposeful life to be experienced in Jesus' eternal Kingdom. Let's turn our attention to the eternal lifestyle of those kingdom people. In turn this lifestyle reveals how we can discover goals for growing our lives in this world so that we can more fully enjoy now and forever. God set this lifestyle for what is good, pleasing and perfect for all humanity. Learning to live as God intends involves discovering God's will and plan for each person. In His amazing creation of diversity, God's plan contains specific situations for each person that shape him or her into a uniquely designed character. However, the general traits of God's will for the human lifestyle remain the same for everyone.

Jesus began His great prayer with this verse in Matthew 6:9-10 (NIV) *"Our Father in heaven, may Your name be kept holy. May Your Kingdom come soon. May Your will be done on earth, as it is in heaven."* As Jesus led His followers into a close relationship with God the Father, He taught them to keep the Father's name holy. Keeping God's name holy means far more than misusing that name by swearing. Jesus wants His disciples who bear the name of the Son of God – Christians - to live so that everything they say and do honors God. Last chapter, we learned that worship is the number one purpose of God's eternal people. We also learned that by glorifying God we enjoy Him. When we honor God in our daily words and actions, we worship Him and keep His name holy. In doing so, we mature as His holy people through the power of the Holy Spirit. Keeping God's name holy is the prime witness and worship of followers of Jesus in glorifying Him.

Jesus immediately follows up that sentence with the petition that God's Kingdom comes soon. Why? Because in the eternal Kingdom, God's name is kept holy through each action and utterance of every citizen. This results in the joy of living for God's glory. How will that happen? Jesus told His disciples that happens when God's will is *"done on earth as it is in heaven."* The Kingdom of God arrives in great force when those on earth try do just as much as those in heaven to keep God's name holy. In His eternal Kingdom, God's will is done completely and fully as God the Father is always honored. By living in God's will, all exist in the peaceful harmony with no harm to any and with all good for all.

The Apostle Paul explained that God's will is always *"good, pleasing and perfect"* in Romans 12:2. Note the important conjunctive 'and'. It is not that God's will is good sometimes, pleasing at other times, or perfect every once in a while. Life in the eternal kingdom will be good, pleasing and perfect all the time. In this life, we tend to think that what is good for us is not very pleasing. So many of the sweet things that taste good, dieticians tell us not to eat. Many things that don't have much taste or don't taste well, we are told to eat. In this kind of thinking, some feel doing God's will is like being told by your parents to eat your vegetables because they are 'good' for you. Thus, they think that God's good will must be endured by doing things that we don't like and to do that which we must learn to like. (Let me digress for a moment to help make this understandable.) We are often told to eat lots of vegetables. But I don't like some vegetables such as Brussels sprouts, kale or cauliflower. People tell me how to prepare these vegetables in a way I might like them. Why should we eat somethings when we need to mask their bitter taste so that we can enjoy them? That makes no sense to me and it still does not taste good. That it is often how people think about God's will as something not enjoyable but must be lived out. However, that's not the 'good' will of Jesus' prayer or Paul's teaching of God's will. His will is good and pleasing to us. It is pleasing and perfect for us. It is all three; good, pleasing and perfect.

God's will is never bad for us. God's will does not lead us toward wrong actions or give us an excuse to promote bad things. When we do the things the Lord asks of us, we find them good, pleasing and perfect. Good is not defined by what humanity thinks is good, but what the Lord says is good. God designed us to live in specific ways. He knows what makes life enjoyable and what makes us feel good. When we live out God's will for our lives, we find joy, meaning and purpose; greater than we ever thought possible. Jesus affirms that doing the will of His Father is the lifestyle of heaven in Matthew 12:50 **(NIV)** *"Anyone who does the will of My Father in heaven is My brother and sister and mother!"* Heavenly people do the will of the Father. In living by the Father's will, they are family to Jesus; one truly big, happy, eternal family.

Living eternally in God's will produces a spiritual lifestyle marked by the fruit of the Holy Spirit. Galatians 5:22-23 describes the benefits that result from this spiritual, eternal lifestyle. (NIV) *"But the fruit of the Spirit is love, joy, peace, patience, kindness, goodness, faithfulness, gentleness and self-control. Against such things there is no law."* Who would tell anyone not to enjoy apples, oranges, cherries, and so many wonderful berries? Who does not want more love, joy, peace, patience and all the rest of these sweet spiritual fruit in their lives? Who would make a law against this wonderful spiritual fruit? This is the lifestyle of God's Kingdom - always treating one another with these sweet behaviors because the Holy Spirit flows unhindered through all relationships. These behaviors describe the normal, regular, good, pleasing and perfect lifestyle of those who live in the eternal

Kingdom.

Living in the Holy Spirit brings a great deepening in maturity in relationships. The more we practice these behaviors in our lives, the more we grow toward greater love together. Love is unending as it never stops, fails or ends. As God is love and as God is infinite and eternal, love is infinite and eternal. The people of His Kingdom will always grow in all the fruit of the Spirit - more love, more joy, more peace, etc. There will be no hate. All will show love in the eternal kingdom, but they will be able to mature in it – to deepen it.

Our culture makes a big deal of Valentine's Day (maybe too big a deal?). That seems to be the only day on which love gets recognized. True love is vital all the time. I watched a TV reporter interview people coming to a flower market on Valentine's Day. He found a young man with 100 roses he bought for his girlfriend. This younger man kept smiling. He looked really happy to be taking all those roses to her. It did not matter that he had just spend $200. He thought the price worth the gift. He wanted to see her enjoy them. The newscaster kept making fun of the young man because he was *"making the rest of us look bad."* No, that young man was in love. Love sacrifices because love finds great joy in sharing with others.

Then, the newsman found a couple waiting to go in the flower shop who have been buying flowers together all the 21 years of their marriage. The newscaster said, *"Congratulations, you must be doing something right."* For them, this was not such a big deal. They showed love yearly on Valentine's Day because they show love to each other every day. They loved to be in love. The newsman had a hard time understanding that concept. He had a hard time understanding that couple and the young man. Many marriages don't last because couples won't sacrifice in love for each other and discover the deeper relationship. My wife and I will soon celebrate 40 years of marriage. Let me tell you a secret. I am still learning how to really love. I'm not perfect in love by a long way.

There are many times when I still fail to love as she deserves. Yet the love I experience now with her is so much greater than the love I knew 40 years ago. I am enjoying it more now than ever before.

Love deepens forever in the eternal Kingdom relationships due to the infinite love of the Lord Jesus. After 100 years in that eternal Kingdom, love still matures. After 1,000 years in that eternal Kingdom, greater joy and peace keep surpassing all understanding. After 100,000 years, kindness, faithfulness and gentleness keep progressing. After a million years, goodness keeps on growing. The infinite Father keeps filling His finite children with more and more of the good, pleasing and perfect life. That loving life will remain satisfying and joyful for eternity.

There is one characteristic of the eternal lifestyle that we can learn to practice now for deeper relationships. That characteristic is speaking the truth in unconditional and sacrificial love. Many teach that we are to *"speak the truth in love"*, but I want to emphasize that the love mentioned here is unconditional and sacrificial love, the 'agape' love of Jesus. The Apostle Paul wrote about this vital, eternal lifestyle characteristic as the very definition of maturity in Ephesians 4:13-15. (NIV) "*...until we all reach unity in the faith and in the knowledge of the Son of God and become mature, attaining to the whole measure of the fullness of Christ. Then we will no longer be infants, tossed back and forth by the waves, and blown here and there by every wind of teaching and by the cunning and craftiness of people in their deceitful scheming. Instead, **speaking the truth in love**, we will grow to become in every respect the mature body of Him who is the head, that is, Christ.*"

The Bible defines maturity as the fullness of Christ in us. That is the end goal of God's desire for humanity. Followers of Jesus become like Him in their lifestyles. When this happens, no childish foolishness, no faddish waffling, no false teaching and no deceitful scheming occurs among God's people. Those are the characteristics of those who are still infantile in their lifestyles.

Maturity in Christ produces steadfastness, faithfulness, and a peaceful calmness in the midst of any storm. The maturity of Christ in us is most clearly displayed, wrote Paul, when we have attained the highest of behaviors together – to always speak the truth in 'agape' love to each other. That will happen in the eternal Kingdom, but we can still work on learning how to mature in that love now. If we do so, our unity and love together will grow faster than it is doing now. Therefore, let us be sure we understand what speaking the truth in 'agape' love really means.

Speaking the truth in 'agape' love means never putting anyone down but lifting the other person to the Lord. Most often, people understand this to mean that we must love another enough to speak the truth even if its uncomfortable. We share our concerns with others when we see them doing or saying something which is not of the Lord, which harms others or themselves. This is true, but remember that we confront them only in love, not with a big stick of judgment that harms them. We must speak the truth in 'agape' love with another in mutual grace, knowing that we need the same grace in return. Sometimes, speaking the truth in 'agape' love means staying quiet until we can figure out how to speak that truth in love. Both truth and love must be present all the time to truly speak the truth in 'agape' love. We learn to be truthful in how we love – not by watering truth down but by applying it correctly. Some people confuse love with being nice and tolerant. They don't want to confront anyone – just let them be and hope they learn for themselves or that someone else will talk to them. That is not 'agape' love as it does not help the other person to grow in the truth. That is cowardly avoiding the truth. And make sure you know the truth before you speak it. Most of the time, we misunderstand what really happened and what were the real motivations of others. If you take time to listen first, that will help you know how to speak the truth in 'agape' love.

Speaking the truth in 'agape' love means there is no condemnation, because (NIV) *"there is no condemnation for those who are in*

Christ Jesus" (Romans 8:3). The desire is for correction, not condemnation. Church people today are seen as judgmental because they too often condemn. Listen to the way church people talk about those outside the church. Often, they speak with harsh, judgmental words – not what the Lord desires. Even worse, I have heard too many in churches speak ill of others in the fellowship of Jesus. Such behavior has no place in the true Church of Jesus Christ. Nathan Busenitz of Ligonier Ministries ("Speaking the Truth in Love") wrote *"Speaking the truth in love addresses the way in which we speak. We must not be obnoxious with the truth, or personally offensive in how we approach others. Rather, we are called to communicate in such a way that the manner of our speaking honors our Lord Jesus and edifies His body, the church."*

Speaking the truth in 'agape' love requires a desire to help others – to draw them closer to the Lord. Tony Reinke (senior writer for DesiringGod.org, "Speaking the Truth in Love") wrote, *"At its core, we speak the truth in love when we care enough to speak the gospel into the lives of those around us. This is God's everyday calling for every Christian."* Speaking the truth in love truly will be unconditional in the eternal Kingdom. Too often we dare to try to love deeply only those we want to love in this world. Our love must broaden its objects greatly. In heaven, we will love each other – everyone in heaven. The more we can learn how to speak the truth in sacrificial, unconditional love – the love Jesus has for us – the more that Jesus' true church can grow among us, and so that we are better prepared for the lifestyle of God's eternal Kingdom.

Jesus summed up the vital truth to an eternal lifestyle when He had this conversation with a teacher of the law of God in Mark 12:28-34.
"One of the teachers of the law came and heard them debating. Noticing that Jesus had given them a good answer, he asked Him, 'Of all the commandments, which is the most important?'
'The most important one,' answered Jesus, 'is this: "Hear, O Israel, the Lord our God, the Lord is one. Love the Lord your God with all your

heart and with all your soul and with all your mind and with all your strength." The second is this: "Love your neighbor as yourself." There is no commandment greater than these.'"
'Well said, teacher,' the man replied. 'You are right in saying that God is one and there is no other but Him. To love Him with all your heart, with all your understanding and with all your strength, and to love your neighbor as yourself is more important than all burnt offerings and sacrifices.'
When Jesus saw that he had answered wisely, He said to him, 'You are not far from the kingdom of God.'"

Kingdom people, whether they are learning how to relate to others in this world or as they will relate for eternity, try to love God with all their heart, soul, mind and strength, and to love each other fully. As we learn to live in the greatest of all commandments, the fullness of God's will for each one, we prepare ourselves for the lifestyle that brings wonderful and richly rewarding relationships in the eternal Kingdom of God.

ETERNAL LIFE EARTH

Life on the New Earth

Key questions addressed in this chapter:
- Where is heaven – above this earth?
- Will there be natural calamities in heaven such as earthquakes or tornadoes?
- Will there be mosquitos and other pests in heaven?
- Will there be mountains and oceans to enjoy in heaven?

Where is heaven? Is heaven above in the sky? It depends on how you define heaven. The Bible has 2 different definitions for heaven. The first definition of heaven is the place where God lives. By this definition, heaven is not a place above, below or beside us. The dwelling place of God cannot be contained by human dimensions, for the unlimited God cannot be restrained by time or space. When the Bible described Jesus ascending to His Father in heaven, it meant He went beyond the senses of his 3-dimensional followers into the presence of God the Father. The second way the Bible talks about heaven is as the space that contains the sun, moon and stars that we look up to each day and night. So, by this second definition - yes, the heavens are up above us.

This is important in understanding eternal life because it concerns where the people of God will live forever. Will they live in heaven or on earth? The Bible talks about Jesus' followers living with Him in heaven. So where will that heaven be? Will Jesus' followers live in the unlimited dimensions of God's heaven? No. Followers of Jesus, as we made clear before in describing eternal life bodies, don't become gods with unlimited spiritual and physical presence; what theologians call omnipresent. They have eternal bodies that don't wear out, but they will still exist in space and time dimensions. They will live in these limited dimensions under the new heavens, and interestingly enough, on a new earth. We know this because of this second way of defining of heaven. This is found in the Bible's descriptions of what happens to the heavens and earth on the last day, and of the new heaven and earth that occur afterward. Let's look at 2 instances of this in 2nd Peter and then in the Book of Revelation. While examining these verses, we can learn what that place will be like.

2 Peter 3:10-13 (NIV) "*But the day of the Lord will come like a thief. The heavens will disappear with a roar; the elements will be destroyed by fire, and the earth and everything done in it will be laid bare. Since everything will be destroyed in this way, what kind of people ought you to be? You ought to live holy and godly lives as you look forward to the day of God and speed its coming. That day will bring about the destruction of the heavens by fire, and the elements will melt in the heat. But in keeping with His promise we are looking forward to a new heaven and a new earth, where righteousness dwells.*" These verses refer to the second definition of heaven because the old heaven disappears in destruction along with the desolation of the old earth. God's home could never suffer such annihilation as its elements are eternal. In these verses, the heavens and earth melt away, showing them to be the temporal heavens above and the earth below of human dimensions of time and space.

Why must these temporal heavens and earth suffer destruction? The answer goes back to the creation of the universe and world by God. God created the physical heaven and earth for the good and rule of the first humans. As created in God's image, humans were to rule over the creation as His stewards (managers) of the place. The earth would benefit from their virtuous caring as they kept all things on earth in order and harmony. However, when the first humans rebelled against God, in association with the rebellion of Satan and his demons, the heavens and the earth became subjected to their decay and corruption. As the earth would have benefited from proper human care, so it suffered the consequences of evil intent and neglect. Look at the earth's suffering since then from pollution and destruction at the hands of fallen humans. Nature's decline in the pollution of its waters, the ravishing of its features, and the poisoning of its atmosphere is abundantly clear. As a boy living in Anaheim in the 1950s, I never saw smog. By my twenties living in Pasadena in the 1970s, many days I could not see more than a few blocks and rarely saw the mountains a few miles away. The smog now creeps up into the High Desert beyond the mountains and well out into the surrounding deserts. Over 150 million trees in the mountains of California are dead or dying from the pine bark beetle infestation. In the Southern Sierra Nevada mountain range, the percentage of trees dying is estimated at 80%. Whole mountainsides reveal nothing but brown, dead tree trunks in many western states. Beneath the waters of San Francisco Bay lies a layer of silt, mud and mercury poisoning washed down by the goldminers of the 1850s. An enlarging trash heap of plastics revolves out in the middle of the Pacific Ocean. A growing trash belt grows in orbit around the earth of broken and discarded satellites, rockets and other jetsam sent out by humans. These are a few of the many problems created by humans who care little for what happens to our earth, sea and skies.

The Apostle Paul wrote of this earthly and heavenly corruption in Romans 8:19-21, and of the hope for its liberation. (NIV) *"For the creation waits in eager expectation for the children of God to be revealed. For the creation was subjected to frustration, not by its own choice, but by the will of the One who subjected it, in hope that the creation itself will be liberated from its bondage to decay and brought into the freedom and glory of the children of God."* This means that the true children of God and the true angelic and spiritual creatures who serve God will have an uncorrupted and pure residence (as Peter wrote *where righteousness dwells*). The old heavens and earth must be replaced in fiery purification of all evil and corruption. A new heaven and earth will provide a place with no pollution, corruption or disorder, and where all live in perfection of harmony and purpose.

Revelation 21:1-4 explains this new heaven and earth. (NIV) *"Then I saw a new heaven and a new earth, for the first heaven and the first earth had passed away, and there was no longer any sea. I saw the Holy City, the new Jerusalem, coming down out of heaven from God, prepared as a bride beautifully dressed for her husband. And I heard a loud voice from the throne saying, 'Now the dwelling of God is with men, and He will live with them. They will be His people, and God Himself will be with them and be their God. He will wipe every tear from their eyes. There will be no more death or mourning or crying or pain, for the old order of things has passed away.'"*

A new heaven and a new earth will be the place for the eternal people of God. This will be their new home in which they play, work and enjoy every day, with a whole new universe ready to explore. The earth below and the skies above exist for the glory of God and the abundant life of His people. In this place, no death, mourning, crying or pain exist. In this place, not one tear is shed. In this place, life thrives.

Verse 1 contains an interesting fact about the new earth in that it will not have any sea. What does that mean? That there are no seas bothers many who love the sea. They worry that means there will be no waves to surf or oceans to sail. They get saddened if that means there will be no dolphins, whales or any of the amazing creatures of the sea. They get upset that this might mean we won't be able to walk the beaches and hear the roar of the surf. It is hard to tell what this means because this fact is not mentioned elsewhere in the Bible. We can only take our best guess at what it means. I will share my thoughts about this with you; with the understanding that it is only my best guess, not a fact that I know for sure. You and others are free to disagree with me if you have another and better explanation, as others have proposed.

In my best thinking about the lack of seas in the future earth, I take it to mean that there will be no briny or alkaline waters; no salty waters that cannot refresh our thirst. The Salton Sea spreads out in the desert of Southern California. The Salton Sea exists due to a human mistake when the fresh waters of the Colorado River were inadvertently redirected. For many months those waters flowed into and filled up a low spot in the desert below the Palm Springs area. Without more fresh water to refill it and without any outlet, the fresh water evaporated down over the years to become briny and polluted. At first it became a nature preserve for tens of thousands of birds. Now it has become a killing zone for them. The seas of this earth have that quality of death and decay. Everything empties into them. They need to be renewed.

The salt water 'seas' of this world represent the corruption and chaos of creation in this broken world. In the new earth, the waters will be full of life and freshness. I believe that the incredible diversity of life we see in this world, from the imaginative creativity of God, will be magnified, not lost, in the eternal earth and heavens. The fresh waters of the new world will team with dolphins, whales and all sorts of amazing creatures, even though they will be fresh not salty. God will enable His creatures to adapt. There will be waves to surf and bodies of water to sail. Why not? It just won't be salty, briny, alkaline or harmful to anyone or anything. However, it may not be so vast as our present oceans so that the new earth can contain all of the large family of God's eternal people.

The biggest fact to discover of the new heaven and earth is that the barrier between the dwelling place of God and the dwelling place of His human followers will be no more. God will 'descend' from His eternal, unlimited Heavenly dwelling and live among His people on the new earth. Since heaven is the dwelling place of God, and as God will live among His people on the new earth, the new earth becomes the new center of heaven for His eternal kingdom. The Biblical definitions of heaven merge into one as the God Incarnate dwells among His people. There they see Him, interact with Him, be healed and renewed to abundant life with Him. Everything of God is resurrected to new. The followers of Jesus become God's children and citizens of His great eternal Kingdom. (Next chapter I will explain more of the new Jerusalem mentioned here in these verses.

A few more glimpses of the new earth appear as the dwelling place of God with His eternal people in Revelation 7:14-17 (NIV) *"And he said, 'These are they who have come out of the great tribulation; they have washed their robes and made them white in the blood of the Lamb. Therefore, "they are before the throne of God and serve Him day and night in His temple; and He who sits on the throne will spread His tent over them. Never again will they hunger; never again will they thirst. The sun will not beat upon them, nor any scorching heat. For the Lamb at the center of the throne will be their shepherd; He will lead them to springs of living water. And God will wipe away every tear from their eyes.'"* These verses affirm the healing of God for His eternal people, and how living with Him will create a place of abundant life with fresh, life-giving water. The Lamb of God, the Lord Jesus, lives among them. He is the Good Shepherd who cares for all their needs and leads them to the great blessings of God's Kingdom. He makes sure everything is in balance. The sun will not beat on them with scorching heat. The Lord provides the air conditioning with His *'tent'* (His covering of protection) spread out over them. (Notice there is a sun mentioned here in the eternal Kingdom.) I feel I can also affirm that, as the heat will not scorch, so also the cold will not bite under this protection of Christ as He controls the climate of the new world. There will be no hunger or thirst there. The Good Shepherd provides for all the Springs of living water and the Bread of life as Jesus promised in John 6:35 and in John 7:38. The Lord wipes away all tears forever, restoring joy to each one. Those who suffered persecution in this world receive special honor and joy in the next as they serve before the Lord each day and night. Each of these descriptions build up an understanding of life in the presence of the Lord Jesus that will be forever full of meaning and satisfaction. This is a place to look forward to living with God and others in wonderful enjoyment.

Let's refer back to Romans 8:20-21 as it reveals more gems to share about eternal life. (NIV) *"For the creation was subjected to frustration, not by its own choice, but by the will of the One who subjected it, in hope that the creation itself will be liberated from its bondage to decay and brought into the freedom and glory of the children of God."* The bondage to decay of this earth, due to the rebellion against God, resulted in a world out of harmony with the original intention of God's created order. As nature went out of balance, it caused what are called 'natural calamities' such as earthquakes, tornadoes, hurricanes, floods, drought, blizzards, intense heat or cold, and other extremes of peril to life. In the Biblical reality, these are not natural calamities, but "broken nature" calamities. If I have an appliance working well such as a washing machine, I have no problems with it. But get that washing machine out of whack with an uneven load and you get all kinds of noise and possible breakdowns. In a more devastating way, the earth is out of whack – off balance, and needs to be righted.

The new earth will be liberated from the old earth's bondage to decay and restored to a perfect balance with the Lord and His people. It will be a place of proper restraints on its natural boundaries to support life, not to cause harm. There will be snow on the mountains to play in, but no damaging frost to the plants. There will be amazing geothermal geysers and volcanic displays, but no explosive destruction (think not of a Mt. St. Helens outburst but more of a Hawaiian slow flow that builds islands like at Kīlauea). There will be refreshing rains but not torrential downpours. There will be softly blowing breezes but not unchecked windstorms. There will be no more natural catastrophes, but plenty of natural wonder.

From this discussion of harmful natural catastrophes being brought back into healthy boundaries, we can also address another vexing question. Many wonder if there will be mosquitos in heaven? The question can be much further enlarged. Will there be ticks, fire ants, spiders, chiggers, horse flies, and innumerable other harmful or bothersome pests? While the Bible does not say what happens to these 'pest' species, we can affirm the following that leads to some possible answers. First, the Bible shares that no harm or suffering exists in the eternal kingdom. Thus, if they do exist in the eternal Kingdom, these animals will not bring any problem to the humans there. Second, we described how the Bible notes there will be snakes, even what were poisonous ones, in the new Kingdom. But these do not harm even a young child there. (Isaiah 11:6-9) Thus, any animal that exists now as a threat or cause of harm or discomfort to humans will not be a problem. Third, we realize that everything finds its proper place in balance and harmony in God's eternal Kingdom. So, although we cannot say for sure if mosquitos or other such pests will certainly or not exist in heaven, we can say that if they do exist, they will fit in well with all other animals and have a divine purpose for being there. They will not cause any harm or suffering but add to the amazing wonder and diversity of all of God's creatures.

The new earth and heavens will contain places beneficial to life and full of amazing exploration: slot canyons and grand canyons, tall peaks and rolling hills, rich forests and waving grasslands, refreshing waterfalls, streams and lakes, stars uncountable above our heads, and sand pebbles innumerable bellow our toes on long, gorgeous beaches. Think of the most beautiful spot on this earth that you have ever experienced. Now realize that the wonders of the new heavens and earth will be so much more than you and I can ever imagine. I once thought I would never find a more beautiful place than the Colorado Rocky Mountains. Then I saw the Alaskan Range and Mt. Denali, more magnificent than anywhere in the Rockies or the Sierra Nevadas. Even more, the majesty of the wonders of the new world will reward us with greater wonder and joy.

All this and more will fill the place called home for the people of the eternal Kingdom of God. As the people of God's Kingdom will have eternal bodies with amazing new capabilities, so they will have an eternal earth and heavens to explore and enjoy with those bodies. We have so much to look forward to if we follow the Lord Jesus Christ as our Savior and Lord into His eternal Kingdom.

ETERNAL LIFE DWELLINGS

Life in the City of God

Key questions addressed in this chapter:
- Will everyone get a mansion in heaven?
- What will eternal dwelling places be like in heaven and what will they be constructed with?
- What is so important about a new Jerusalem?
- Will there be stars, moon and a sun in heaven?

Do you expect to have a mansion in heaven? According to the King James Version, that is what Jesus promised His followers. The trouble with that translation is that the original Greek language does not promise mansions. The best translation means a place, room or dwelling in the Father's house. Here is what Jesus really said as found in *John 14:2 (NIV) "In My Father's house are many rooms; if it were not so, I would have told you. I am going there to prepare a place for you."*

I'm sorry if you feel let down, but you don't really have to feel that way. When we consider the amazing generosity of God the Father and all we have already discovered of the riches awaiting those who will live in His eternal Kingdom, we must conclude that a room in His house must be very cozy and nice indeed. That room would be much better than enjoying a room at the White House or Buckingham Palace. Every room in the house of the Almighty God and Ruler of the Universe must be wonderful; much better than any mansion built here on earth. I guess you will get a mansion-like room after all, if you follow Jesus into His eternal Kingdom.

Every room in the Father's House, personally prepared by Jesus, will be perfect for each one. Isn't it remarkable to know that Jesus is preparing a place for His disciples! He knows just what we need and like. He will give each one a place personally prepared for abundant life. It may well come decorated in the favorite colors, fashions and styles of each person there. The chairs and couches will be plush and comfortable. The beds will indeed be heavenly. Everything we might need or want will be available. How do we know this? Well, in addition to the fact that Jesus prepares the rooms, the description we get of the eternal City of Jerusalem specifies that the finest of precious materials and construction abound throughout every street and building. A very detailed description of the New Jerusalem is found in Revelation 21. The main truth in this passage is the presence of God among His people in the eternal Kingdom. We will take it in parts to better understand this amazing dwelling place for God and His people in the new earth of the eternal Kingdom.

Revelation 21:10-11 (NIV) *"And he carried me away in the Spirit to a mountain great and high, and showed me the Holy City, Jerusalem, coming down out of heaven from God. It shone with the glory of God, and its brilliance was like that of a very precious jewel, like a jasper, clear as crystal."*

Throughout the Bible, there are hints that the Temple in Jerusalem was an earthly copy of the much greater House of God in heaven. For instance, after speaking about priests serving at the Temple on earth, Hebrews 8:5 states this (NIV) *"They serve at a sanctuary that is a copy and shadow of what is in heaven."* All that happened in the Temple in the earthly Jerusalem gave a symbolic glimpse of what truly happens in God's perfect Temple in heaven. All the sacrifices symbolized the great sacrifice Jesus made on the cross. Jesus is the one and only, true, Great High Priest, who intercedes with God the Father on behalf of His people. By His blood, Jesus' followers enter into the eternal Holy of Holies to have fellowship with God the Father. Now this heavenly Jerusalem, the dwelling place of the Most High God, will come down out of heaven to the new earth. God will dwell among His people and they will have access to Him personally through Jesus. And what a presence that will be!

Even though the Bible is the greatest book ever written and read, it is still impossible to describe the radiant majesty of God in human words. So, the Bible does the next best thing – it describes the radiance around God with the best of human words. If the things all around God are amazingly awesome, God is far more awesome above them. In this case the description is of a very rare and priceless jewel, a jasper as clear as crystal. Jasper is a quartz aggregate that occurs in many different colors: usually red, yellow, brown or green depending in the minerals included in its formation. Jaspers adorn the brightest and best rings, necklaces, and crowns of royal persons. A jewel is only as good as the light it reflects. The jasper described in this verse outshone all others with the luminous glow of the light reflecting facets coming from the brilliance of God Himself.

The great and royal eternal City of God comes down to earth with its imposing and formidable walls and dimensions. Revelation 21:12-14 notes (NIV) *"It had a great, high wall with twelve gates, and with twelve angels at the gates. On the gates were written the names of the twelve tribes of Israel. There were three gates on the east, three on the north, three on the south and three on the west. The wall of the city had twelve foundations, and on them were the names of the twelve apostles of the Lamb."* The 4 massive walls with 12 imposing gates enclose the city with an angel standing guard at each gate. The gates commemorate the 12 tribes of Israel. 12 huge foundation stones undergird the walls. Each foundation stone was named for one of the 12 apostles of Jesus, who established His Church forever by carrying out His great commission to make disciples of all nations. These gates and walls will stand forever in the strength and power of the Living Word of God.

Just how massive are the city, gates and walls of the New Jerusalem? The dimensions are listed in Revelation 21:15-17 (NIV) *"The angel who talked with me had a measuring rod of gold to measure the city, its gates and its walls. The city was laid out like a square, as long as it was wide. He measured the city with the rod and found it to be 12,000 stadia in length, and as wide and high as it is long. The angel measured the wall using human measurement, and it was 144 cubits thick."* 12,000 stadia translated into modern measure equates to about 1400 miles. So, this city will be 1400 miles in length, 1400 miles in width and 1400 miles in height - a perfect, massive cube! Remember that the Holy of Holies room of the earthly Temple where God was said to dwell was a perfect cube too. Yet this 'Holy of Holies' coming down from heaven to earth is an immense dwelling place for God Almighty. If we were to place this city on the West Coast of the United States, it would stretch east from San Francisco past Denver, Colorado into Kansas and Oklahoma, and north from San Diego above Vancouver, Canada. Basically, this one City of God would cover the entire western half of the lower 48 states. And the walls themselves will be very thick – 144 cubits translates into 200-foot-thick, massive walls, 2/3 the size of a football field!

These walls convey the majestic splendor of God as described in Revelation 21:18-21 (NIV) *"The wall was made of jasper, and the city of pure gold, as pure as glass. The foundations of the city walls were decorated with every kind of precious stone. The first foundation was jasper, the second sapphire, the third chalcedony, the fourth emerald, the fifth sardonyx, the sixth carnelian, the seventh chrysolite, the eighth beryl, the ninth topaz, the tenth chrysoprase, the eleventh jacinth, and the twelfth amethyst. The twelve gates were twelve pearls, each gate made of a single pearl. The great street of the city was of pure gold, like transparent glass."* The walls consist of invaluable gemstones. The gates are made from immense single pearls. Pure gold forms the construction material of the city behind those walls and gates. Are you getting the picture of a place of indescribable magnificence? I hope so, because that is the intent of the author. This eternal city must be grand and glorious enough to be the home of the King of kings.

God is more amazingly luminous and radiant than the whole city.

Hear about this in Revelation 21:22-27 (NIV) *"I did not see a temple in the city, because the Lord God Almighty and the Lamb are its temple. The city does not need the sun or the moon to shine on it, for the glory of God gives it light, and the Lamb is its lamp. The nations will walk by its light, and the kings of the earth will bring their splendor into it. On no day will its gates ever be shut, for there will be no night there. The glory and honor of the nations will be brought into it. Nothing impure will ever enter it, nor will anyone who does what is shameful or deceitful, but only those whose names are written in the Lamb's book of life."*

A sun, moon and stars will shine in the new heavens of the new earth. However, with God living among His people, their light will not be needed. He outshines them all, so that they are but a dim light above, like when the moon rises up during the day. Every nation and every ruler of the new earth brings their gifts of praise and honor to the Lord God Almighty and the Lamb who sit in this capitol of the new earth. The gates of this city stand wide open 24/7 to God's people. All will live in purity and righteousness before and around this amazing God among them. Not every one of them will live in this great city of God, but all will have access to that city and to God. There will be an entirely beautiful new world to spread out and enjoy.

So, let me ask you an important question - if the building materials of the streets and walls of the Kingdom are gold, crystals and precious stones, what can we expect of the homes and places for God's eternal citizens? Jesus prepares for His faithful followers a dwelling place in His Father's House in the New City of Jerusalem on the new earth. Those homes will be amazing in every aspect of life: relationships, joy, meaning and purpose forever.

Here is one more glimpse the Bible provides of the new Jerusalem as found in Joel 3:17-18 (NIV) *"Then you will know that I, the LORD your God, dwell in Zion, My holy hill. Jerusalem will be holy; never again will foreigners invade her. In that day the mountains will drip new wine, and the hills will flow with milk; all the ravines of Judah will run with water. A fountain will flow out of the LORD'S house and will water the valley of acacias."* A land flowing with wine and milk means this is a land with abundant water. Wine comes from lush vines. Milk comes from sated dairy cows. The hills of Judah in Israel today are a lot like the hills of Southern California that often sit parched and empty of water in their stream beds. During a time of drought, the vineyards of Temecula in Southern California had to cut back on growing their vines and wine became scarce. God promises a land where the ravines and canyons run full with life-giving water. Milk and wine, honey and bread for all abound in God's eternal City. Luscious and green vegetation grow abundantly. Even the deserts become expanses of thirst-quenching water in the new earth of the eternal Kingdom.

Consequently, what does all this mean for us today? If the Lord prepares such a place of light, purity and glory for us to enjoy in the future, we don't have to worry about tomorrow. Jesus said it this way in Matthew 6:33-34 (NIV) *"Seek first His kingdom and His righteousness, and all these things will be given to you as well. Therefore do not worry about tomorrow, for tomorrow will worry about itself. Each day has enough trouble of its own."* For every follower of Jesus, the future is secure and wonderful. So, we can focus on what can we do in our lives in this world to shine more for the Lord's glory to those around us. We can spend our time doing the things God wants us to do today for greater life with and for Him. Seek the Lord! Call on Him! Live out His good, pleasing and perfect will for each of your days. All of this will prepare you for the eternal blessings and rewards that come from having faith in Jesus Christ today.

ETERNAL LIFE REWARDS

The Benefits of Life with God

Key questions addressed in this chapter:
- Are there rewards and treasures in heaven for good things done on this earth?
- What gain is there eternally for any sacrifice people make in this life?
- Why does Jesus encourage and warn us that the first will be last and the last will be first in the Kingdom of Heaven?

I write this chapter with some trepidation. I fear that some will misunderstand my words to mean that we can in some way earn our way into heaven by a reward system for our deeds. So, let me clearly dispel that notion. No one can earn their own way into heaven. All need to be cleansed and transformed to enjoy eternal love, joy and peace. Salvation comes only by grace received through faith in the name of Jesus. However, the New Testament includes many references to some type of reward system for those who do enter into the eternal Kingdom. Thus, we do well to look into these rewards and explain why they are important to followers of Jesus.

Credit card companies know people usually have a number of cards to choose from, but they want you to use their cards. To encourage you to use their card, they offer lucrative rewards programs. I discovered that by using one of my credit cards almost exclusively I can get better rewards. I use a card that gives me a lot of points towards free hotel nights. Then, my wife uses a different credit card that gives her many airplane miles. Between the 2 of us, we get inexpensive vacation weeks using these two cards for travel and lodging, we just pay for meals and entertainment.

Humans like rewards. We like to be encouraged and motivated

through rewards and appreciation. God created us that way because He likes to encourage and reward us. So, it should come as no surprise that He has the most amazing reward program to encourage us to do good things. And the amazing thing is that He rewards us even though we should be doing those wholesome things anyway. This reward program is totally free to enter. There is no upfront or annual fee to enter God's reward program. No credit check is required. No minimum FICO score is needed. Jesus told us His reward program is open to anyone. And, like most credit card reward programs, the more you use it, the greater the rewards. Many people are not aware of this amazing heavenly reward program. Let's discuss it so that you can take more advantage of it.

Jesus explained the basic heavenly reward program in Matthew 5:19 (NLT). *"So if you ignore the least commandment and teach others to do the same, you will be called the least in the Kingdom of Heaven. But anyone who obeys God's laws and teaches them will be called great in the Kingdom of Heaven."* Jesus was speaking to His followers that day. They left their homes to go out to the hillsides above Lake Galilee where He was speaking. They showed faith in Him by following Him. As I wrote, with faith in Jesus, following Him as Lord and Savior, anyone can enter into the Kingdom of Heaven. (I will talk more about this next chapter as I address the question – "Who can enter into the Kingdom of Heaven?") In this passage, Jesus shared that if His followers ignored His teaching, they would be in the Kingdom of Heaven, but would gain nothing more. They would be called least in the Kingdom of Heaven. Jesus wanted to encourage His followers to discover more good things from God. So, He told them if they genuinely tried to obey God the Father's commands and follow His teaching, greater rewards would come to them. God honors those who take Him seriously. Jesus rewards those who obey His teaching. The more we obey the teachings of God, the greater will be our rewards in heaven. The only real reward directly mentioned here was the honor to be called 'great' in the Kingdom of Heaven. Yet, as we will see, much more than a title is involved.

Jesus explained more about His reward program in Matthew 19:28-30. (NIV) *Jesus said to them, "I tell you the truth, at the renewal of all things, when the Son of Man sits on His glorious throne, you who have followed Me will also sit on twelve thrones, judging the twelve tribes of Israel. And everyone who has left houses or brothers or sisters or father or mother or children or fields for My sake will receive a hundred times as much and will inherit eternal life. But many who are first will be last, and many who are last will be first."* In the eternal Kingdom everything will be renewed. All debts will be paid, and all sins will be removed. Everyone in that Kingdom will begin again with nothing negative, but with so many positives by merely entering into that place and time. However, some will enter into the Kingdom with even more positives added for them. We know how this works with our credit card rewards. Everyone will be in the grand hotel, but some will get upgraded to suites. Everyone will get on the plane, but some will sit in upgraded comfort seats or first class.

The faithful Apostles who followed Jesus, shared His Word, established His Kingdom throughout the world, and gave up their lives for Him will be given the highest rewards. They will sit next to Jesus' throne. They will help Him officiate over the people of God. Then, spread out next to the Apostles are those who sacrificed for Jesus. Whoever gave up anything for Jesus gets a reward depending on how much they gave up. The more they gave up, the greater the benefits they receive. If they gave up their lives for Jesus (those we call 'martyrs'), they will be greatly honored in the eternal Kingdom and serve Jesus' directly. After that ultimate sacrifice, the greater the sacrifice a follower of Jesus gave for Him, he or she will find their seat closer to Him.

At fancy state dinners in the White House, seating depends on those being honored. The greater the honor, the closer one sits to the President. It is a tremendous honor just to attend a Presidential Banquet, as so few get the opportunity. However, those in attendance find their seats closer to the President based on their achievements or status. So it is with those who sit down with Jesus. The degree to which a follower of Jesus obeyed God's truth and sacrificed for Him in this world determines his or her reward in His Kingdom.

Depending on how much they gave up for Jesus, His followers find greater or lesser gains. Those who gave up homes by following Jesus to other lands, like many missionaries have done, will enjoy 100 times better homes in the best locations of the eternal Kingdom. Those who gave up family to follow Jesus find 100 times more brothers, sisters, fathers and mothers in God's eternal family. Those who gave up good lands and fields to follow Jesus get 100 times better lands and fields in eternal life. Those who gave up lucrative positions for Jesus, that would have made them a lot of money with a lot of prestige, will discover 100 times greater eternal riches and honor. Those who served others and gave up their opportunities to be celebrities and stars, receive 100 times more recognition and adulation in the Kingdom of Heaven. You can't lose anything when you give it up for Jesus. He gives it all back compounded a hundred times over. He appreciates all that His followers to for Him.

I hope you are familiar with compound interest in a safe money market account. It can work greatly in your favor. If you invest early in your life and regularly put aside a small portion of your income, you can become a millionaire or better by the time you retire. A $1000 investment earns interest and becomes a $1500 investment. Keep adding to it and a $10,000 investment becomes a $15,000 investment. That $15,000 investment keep compounding daily while you keep adding savings monthly and you eventually have a $100,000 investment. Interest keeps compounding until you retire with over $1,000,000. The earlier you begin, and the more you put into it, the greater the sum of your savings. When you have a lot invested, your money works for you and abundant returns start coming in. You can get to the point where you no longer have to work. You can live nicely off the returns of your investments. Smart money people do this all the time. Even smarter followers of Christ are doing this now with their time, talents and resources to build up amazing eternal rewards. This gratifying reward system compounds and multiplies into huge eternal dividends. Are you a smart investor in Jesus?

However, those who don't invest for eternity, do not find this compounding of benefits. Don't be surprised by the fact that those who gain much in this world, instead of investing in eternal life, will not be famous, great or rewarded in the Kingdom of the Lord. They received their time in the spotlight in this world. The greatest in the God's Kingdom will not be the ones with all the fame in this world, even in church circles. The greatest in the Lord's Kingdom won't necessarily be the famous preachers and evangelists. More likely, according to Jesus' teaching, it will be the ones who quietly and faithfully followed Jesus in this life; obeying His teaching, trusting in Him for their daily needs; all while sacrificing greatly for others in His name. No one now knows much about their lives or names now, but they will be the 'super stars' of heaven. And this is the fascinating part, no one will be upset at this. Everyone will see this as fair and right for them to be so honored. They deserve all they will receive.

Jesus said it this way in Matthew 6:1-4. (NIV) *"Be careful not to practice your righteousness in front of others to be seen by them. If you do, you will have no reward from your Father in heaven. "So when you give to the needy, do not announce it with trumpets, as the hypocrites do in the synagogues and on the streets, to be honored by others. Truly I tell you, they have received their reward in full. But when you give to the needy, do not let your left hand know what your right hand is doing, so that your giving may be in secret. Then your Father, who sees what is done in secret, will reward you."*

Don't be that one who craves the spotlight, who pushes to the front of the line, who brags about His accomplishments, who always wants things her own way, who makes sure everyone else knows how humble he is acting toward others. Be the one who builds others up, listens more than speaks, and cheerfully gives, not because you must but because you want to give. Be the one who seeks out those in need, instead of making friends with the rich and powerful. Let others go first. The sign of a church full of true followers of Jesus is best seen at a church potluck where everyone tries to be last in line and no one overfills their plate; then there is plenty for everyone. Jesus knows who serves others over themselves and thus serve Him, and He rewards them.

The first will be last and the last will be first. Those who give unselfishly will gain, while the selfish will lose. Whatever we give away for Jesus to receive the glory, He gives back multiplied. Anything we try to keep for ourselves, we will certainly lose. As Jesus remarked in Matthew 16:24-27 (NIV) *Then Jesus said to His disciples, "Whoever wants to be My disciple must deny themselves and take up their cross and follow Me For whoever wants to save their life will lose it, but whoever loses their life for Me will find it. What good will it be for someone to gain the whole world, yet forfeit their soul? Or what can anyone give in exchange for their soul? For the Son of Man is going to come in His Father's glory with His angels, and then He will reward each person according to what they have done."* Entering into heaven requires following Jesus instead of following our own way. Above that, the rewards come according to what we do with the life and good things Jesus gives us. The more we use our life and resources to build up the Lord's Kingdom in this earth, the greater rewards we have waiting for us in His eternal Kingdom.

When it comes to eternal life, it is all about Jesus. He came into this world to rescue us. He showed us how to live perfectly with God the Father and with each other. He obeyed God in every way. He gave His live for us. He rose again so that we can believe in Him and follow Him. When we have faith in Jesus, we follow Him into His eternal Kingdom.

Yet, when it comes to gaining God's rewards, that is up to us. The more we take advantage of the wonderful gifts Jesus gives us to serve Him and others, the more we gain in eternity. This is not cruel or unfair. This is God's way of encouraging us. In no way is this reward system competitive. No one receives greater or lesser rewards in comparison to what another person achieves. The rewards are based solely upon what each one does in and with their lives and gifts from God. Maybe this illustration will help to make that point? It is entitled "The Carpenter's House" (author unknown).

"An elderly carpenter was ready to retire. He told his employer-contractor of his plans to leave the house building business and live a more leisurely life with his wife enjoying his extended family. He would miss the paycheck, but he needed to retire. They could get by. The contractor was sorry to see his good worker go and asked if he could build just one more house as a personal favor. The carpenter said yes, but in time it was easy to see that his heart was not in his work. He resorted to shoddy workmanship and used inferior materials. It was an unfortunate way to end his career. When the carpenter finished his work and the builder came to inspect the house, the contractor handed the front-door key to the carpenter. 'This is your house,' he said, 'my gift to you.'"

The resources we receive in this life are to help us glorify God and build up eternal rewards. If we use them whole-heartedly, our reward is greater. If we use them half-heartedly or with any less desire to serve the Lord with our best, we receive fewer and fewer rewards for our efforts. God desires to encourage us with many wonderful rewards in addition to the unmerited gifts He offers to us. Let us consider this carefully before this life is over. Some give their assent to follow Jesus once and then do little more. They become passive followers of Jesus who barely mature, don't change much, or care much for those around them. God does not want passive followers. He wants us to mature in love and truth. God the Father desires us to be more like His Son Jesus so we can become His eternal sons and daughters. He seeks those who will worship Him in energetic spirit and healthy truth for greater life. Those who seek the Lord more in this life discover the greater rewards now and on into eternal life, and God encourages us to do so with these rewards.

The Apostle Paul explained this in 1 Corinthians 3:11-15. (NIV) "*For no one can lay any foundation other than the one already laid, which is Jesus Christ. If anyone builds on this foundation using gold, silver, costly stones, wood, hay or straw, their work will be shown for what it is, because the Day will bring it to light. It will be revealed with fire, and the fire will test the quality of each person's work. If what he has built survives, the builder will receive a reward. If it is burned up, the builder will suffer loss; he himself will be saved, but only as one escaping through the flames."*

Jesus laid down the foundation of life in His righteous work for us by His death on the cross through the empty tomb to eternal life. All who trust in Him as their Savior receive His free gift of the eternal foundation of life. Then we do our part. We take each day and build upon the work of Jesus for us. But the long-term success of our work depends on what materials we use to build on the foundation of life in Jesus. If we use eternal materials given us by God, these eternal materials remain after the Day of the Lord to continue on into eternity. If we use temporary materials of this earth, they will not last. They will burn up in the Last Day's purifying fire in which nothing temporary survives.

So why spend this life wasting the great things Jesus gives you by filling your life with temporary things of this world? Why not build up eternal lives with Jesus' eternal building materials. The wood, hay and straw that quickly burn are the efforts humans make using temporary things to set up earthly fame, fortune and fancies. This is a tragic waste of time, talents and treasures. The gold, silver and costly stones are the efforts we make to serve the Lord, build up His Kingdom, and build up relationships in Christ using His eternal treasures. Jesus greatly rewards those efforts. To the ones who serve the Lord, the Lord says publicly "*Well done, my good and faithful servant.*" To the ones who build up His Kingdom, the Lord gives them more responsibilities in the eternal kingdom in ruling with Him (see the Parable of the Talents in Matthew 25). To the ones who build up relationships in Christ, the Lord shares all His Heavenly family of countless brothers and sisters who cherish and appreciate them forever.

This reward system of God is both a warning and an encouragement. Beware if you don't take the Lord seriously. He knows that you are passively doing very little. So, your reward will also be very little, if anything at all. You will be glad you made it into heaven, because you will escape the flames, but you will bring nothing with you. Take heart those who sacrifice for the Lord and others. The Lord knows what you are doing. He sees what is in your heart and what you do in secret. He wants to encourage you. One day everything will be known, and the Lord will publicly reward you for everything you do for Him. If you do so, you will take into eternity a great many wonderful and eternal treasures by which you will have greater joy and reward. This is all best summed up in the words of our Lord in Matthew 6:19-21. (NIV) *"Do not store up for yourselves treasures on earth, where moths and vermin destroy, and where thieves break in and steal. But store up for yourselves treasures in heaven, where moths and vermin do not destroy, and where thieves do not break in and steal. For where your treasure is, there your heart will be also."*

Are you storing up treasures in heaven? Are you building on the foundation of faith in Jesus with eternal and glorious materials? Or are you wasting your time and talents on earthly, temporary things? Be wise and make the eternal choice every time! Be a smart follower of Jesus and reap the eternal benefits God provides for those who follow and obey Him. Let the reward system of Jesus encourage you to do greater things for the One who gave all for you.

ETERNAL LIFE CITIZENS

Who Will Live Forever?

Key questions addressed in this chapter:
- Who will make it into the eternal Kingdom of God? (As Jesus put it – who will be sheep and who will be goats?)
- What are the standards needed to fulfill in this life to be sure someone will be in heaven?
- Does God grade people on a curve at the final test day?
- Is it possible to go through the motions and look like a faithful Christian, but not really be a follower of Jesus?

Eternal life with Jesus, as we have been discovering through the promises made in the Bible, means: seeing God face to face in amazing worship; not facing any temptations, suffering, evil or death; behaving in right ways for good every moment; enjoying many deep relationships of compassion and encouragement; exploring an incredible new earth and heaven; leading satisfying, purposeful and meaningful lives each day; having bodies full of energy and youthfulness; living in magnificent dwellings of comfort fit for each one personally by Jesus Himself; and so many other tremendous benefits of being a citizen in the Lord's eternal Kingdom. Having examined some of these wonderful things to look forward to (as there are many more yet to be known and experienced), we are left with one big question - will any of us be there? As others have wisely cautioned, we will be surprised by who will be in the Kingdom. Some we expected to be there will not be there, while others we thought would not be there will be there. But the greatest question each of us must ask is - will we be there too?

Each March, many high school seniors wait to hear if they have been accepted to college. They worked hard to keep up their grades. They took the SAT exams. They wrote long essays on why the colleges should accept them. They sent in their applications some time ago. Now, all they can do is wait for letters to come back from the college admission departments. Will they contain a yes or no? Big hopes and dreams ride on those letters. Some open their letters and give out yells and shrieks of joy. Some open their letters and cry or get angry. Hopefully, at least one of the colleges they applied to will send back that letter of acceptance.

Is that what it is like for those who hope for eternal life? What does it take to enter into the Kingdom of God? What are the requirements to get into heaven? If getting into heaven is anything like getting into college, you may have a whole new set of questions to ask about this: Does God use a grading system based on how well people lived in this world? Is there a bell curve so that someone needs to be in the top percentage of good applicants? Does God accept 20%, 45% or less, or more, of all people who ever lived? Are you and I in that top percentage? Is it a matter of how much we contribute of our time, talents and resources to the church? Does God grade us on attendance at worship services? Will those who went to church at just Christmas and Easter get into His Kingdom or do you need to go to church monthly, every other week, or almost every Sunday? How much effort, love, caring, encouragement, reading the Bible, praying, worshipping, evangelizing, serving on church committees, going on mission trips, and bringing potluck dishes are enough to become a citizen of God's Kingdom? Just how loving, patient, kind, good and peaceful does one need to be to enter into heaven?

All of these questions boil down to one big personal question: on what do you base your assurance that you will be allowed to enter into the Lord's Kingdom? Sometimes, it seems that the Bible gives a mixed message on what God requires for acceptance into His Kingdom. On the one hand, some passages suggest that entrance depends on human efforts. Jesus said this in Matthew 16:27 (NIV) *"For the Son of Man is going to come in His Father's glory with His angels, and then He will reward each person according to what they have done."* On the day Jesus returns to earth to judge humanity, Jesus stated that what each person has done determines their rewards. This seems to read that Jesus decides what happens to each of us by what we have done. So, what do we have to do to enter His Kingdom?

Jesus shared a very challenging parable about who gets into His eternal Kingdom in Matthew 25:31-46. Listen to what He taught. (NIV)

"When the Son of Man comes in His glory, and all the angels with Him, He will sit on His glorious throne. All the nations will be gathered before Him, and He will separate the people one from another as a shepherd separates the sheep from the goats. He will put the sheep on His right and the goats on His left.

Then the King will say to those on His right, 'Come, you who are blessed by My Father; take your inheritance, the kingdom prepared for you since the creation of the world. For I was hungry and you gave Me something to eat, I was thirsty and you gave Me something to drink, I was a stranger and you invited Me in, I needed clothes and you clothed Me, I was sick and you looked after Me, I was in prison and you came to visit Me.'

Then the righteous will answer Him, 'Lord, when did we see You hungry and feed You, or thirsty and give You something to drink? *When did we see You a stranger and invite You in, or needing clothes and clothe You? When did we see You sick or in prison and go to visit You?'*

The King will reply, 'Truly I tell you, whatever you did for one of the least of these brothers and sisters of Mine, you did for Me.'

Then He will say to those on His left, 'Depart from Me, you who are cursed, into the eternal fire prepared for the devil and His angels. For I was hungry and you gave Me nothing to eat, I was thirsty and you gave Me nothing to drink, I was a stranger and you did not invite Me in, I needed clothes and you did not clothe Me, I was sick and in prison and you did not look after Me.'

They also will answer, 'Lord, when did we see You hungry or thirsty or a stranger or needing clothes or sick or in prison, and did not help You?'

He will reply, 'Truly I tell you, whatever you did not do for one of the least of these, you did not do for Me.'
Then they will go away to eternal punishment, but the righteous to eternal life."

After hearing Jesus teaching, each of us should ask, *"Am I a sheep or a goat?"* The requirements for passing Jesus' Judgment Day division between sheep and goats depends on how we treated others. To His faithful sheep, Jesus commends them for feeding the hungry, giving drink to the thirsty, inviting in the stranger, clothing the needy, and visiting the sick and imprisoned. To the rejected goats, He bans them from His presence and sends them to eternal fire with the devil for not caring for others in these ways. How would you judge your own life by these standards? Would you let yourself into Jesus' Kingdom based on how well you care for others in need?

However, in the Bible we also hear of a different way to enter into the eternal Kingdom as citizens and family of God members. John 1:12 states this entrance in this way **(NIV)** *"Yet to all who received Him, to those who believed in His name, He gave the right to become children of God"* This passage does not speak about good deeds as a requirement for eternal life. The standards presented in this verse include only receiving and believing in Jesus as the behaviors which give the right to enter His Kingdom. The great reformers would echo the Apostle Paul in Ephesians 2:8-9 stating that (NIV) *"For it is by grace you have been saved, through faith—and this is not from yourselves, it is the gift of God - not by works, so that no one can boast."*

How do we reconcile these 2 seemingly opposite requirements for getting into God's eternal Kingdom? Is it based on our actions toward others or our acceptance and belief in Jesus? There is no mention in the last Bible verses quoted above of behavioral standards. Or maybe there is? What does it mean to truly receive Jesus and believe in His name? What does it mean to have faith in Jesus' grace and follow Him into eternity? Is it possible to go through the motions and look like a faithful Christian, but not really be a follower of Jesus? I believe the Bible clearly teaches that following Jesus by receiving and believing in Him means having a faith that changes us from the inside out, from our hearts to our behaviors.

There are two Bible verses that place these two, seemingly opposing requirements for eternal life with Jesus, back to back. These verses are found in Philippians 2:12-13 (NIV) *"Therefore, my dear friends, as you have always obeyed—not only in my presence, but now much more in my absence—continue to work out your salvation with fear and trembling, for it is God who works in you to will and to act in order to fulfill His good purpose."* Paul first taught us to work out our salvation in our daily lives. Then he wrote that God works our salvation into our lives. Put them together to understand that we work out what God works into us. Faith in Jesus is not a one-time, static thing. Faith in Jesus is a relationship with the living Lord. Once we get to know Jesus, He continues to affect us daily. We decide to receive Jesus and trust Him as our Savior at one time. Then we follow Him as our Lord every day from that point on. A relationship is not a one-time occurrence. A relationship is a continuing involvement. Being a disciple of Jesus – discipleship - is all about 'followship'. Followship means to trust and obey every day in this relationship with Jesus. In trusting and obeying we demonstrate that we live with Jesus as our Lord and Savior.

C. S. Lewis described this seeming paradox in this way *"The Bible really seems to clinch the matter when it puts the two things together into one amazing sentence. The first half is, 'Work out your own salvation with fear and trembling' - which looks as if everything depended on us and our good actions: but the second half goes on, 'For it is God who worketh in you' - which looks as if God did everything and we nothing. I am afraid that is the sort of thing we come up against in Christianity. I am puzzled, but I am not surprised. You see, we are now trying to understand, and to separate into water-tight compartments, what exactly God does and what man does when God and man are working together. And, of course, we begin by thinking it is like two men working together, so that you could say, 'He did this bit and I did that.' But this way of thinking breaks down. God is not like that. He is inside you as well as outside: even if we could understand who did what, I do not think human language could properly express it."* (C. S. Lewis, <u>Mere Christianity</u>, p. 149. HarperCollins. Kindle Edition.)

Jesus completed the work of salvation for us through His death on the cross to remove our sinfulness and then in His victorious victory over death in His resurrection. We cannot add anything to that work of salvation. We don't earn it in any way. It is His free and loving gift of merciful grace to us. Yet, we do need to accept that gift of Jesus' work of salvation into our lives. I could hand you a 100-dollar bill, but if you won't take it from me and use it, it does not help you at all. We need to receive Him and believe in His saving work on our behalf. That means we start a relationship with Him for eternity so that He can work into us what we work out every day. We work with God, not apart from Him. We can't separate what He does and what we do in our daily lives as we work out what He works in. He gives us the Holy Spirit so we can live by the Spirit's wisdom and power. He gives us the Fruit of the Spirit so we can demonstrate His lifestyle in our relationships. He gives us the Gifts of the Spirit so we can carry out the ministry that brings glory to His name. Faith in Jesus means an inevitable change comes in and through our behaviors because Jesus works in and through our lives. Followers of Jesus do works of compassion toward others because they have faith (believe) in Jesus. Without that faith relationship, they could do very little of those good works. The Apostle James stated this in James 2:14-17 (NIV) *"What good is it, my brothers and sisters, if someone claims to have faith but has no deeds? Can such faith save them? Suppose a brother or a sister is without clothes and daily food. If one of you says to them, "Go in peace; keep warm and well fed," but does nothing about their physical needs, what good is it? In the same way, faith by itself, if it is not accompanied by action, is dead."* Real faith proceeds to good works in a living relationship with Jesus. Faith without works is not real believing. (And works without faith is not real receiving.)

Again, C. S. Lewis gave a great explanation of this. *"And, in yet another sense, handing everything over to Christ does not, of course, mean that you stop trying. To trust Him means, of course, trying to do all that He says. There would be no sense in saying you trusted a person if you would not take his advice. Thus, if you have really handed yourself over to Him, it must follow that you are trying to obey Him. But trying in a new way, a less worried way. Not doing these things in order to be saved, but because He has begun to save you already. Not hoping to get to Heaven as a reward for your actions, but inevitably wanting to act in a certain way because a first faint gleam of Heaven is already inside you."* (C. S. Lewis, Mere Christianity, pp. 147-148. Harper-Collins. Kindle Edition)

To believe is to trust in Jesus with our lives. I could show you a bridge over a deep canyon. To get to the other side you would need to step out onto that bridge with your whole weight. You could say you believe the bridge will get you over, but unless you actually step onto that bridge, your statement means nothing. To believe in Jesus means to trust our whole lives in His work of salvation to get us over the gulf that exists between death and new life in His eternal kingdom.

It turns out that the goats never really had any faith. They never trusted and thus never obeyed. And the sheep received their faith when they started following Jesus. They trusted and Jesus led them over into greater life of caring love and active faith into eternity. Be encouraged or beware! One more quote from C. S. Lewis may help us to grasp this truth, when he writes about those who falsely say, since they have faith, it does not matter what they do. *"The other set were accused of saying, 'Faith is all that matters. Consequently, if you have faith, it doesn't matter what you do. Sin away, my lad, and have a good time and Christ will see that it makes no difference in the end.' The answer to that nonsense is that, if what you call your 'faith' in Christ does not involve taking the slightest notice of what He says, then it is not faith at all— not faith or trust in*

Him, but only intellectual acceptance of some theory about Him." (C. S. Lewis, <u>Mere Christianity.</u> p. 148. HarperCollins. Kindle Edition.)

There truly is a correlation between an active faith in Jesus that results in greater good deeds. Those good deeds confirm the original faith that leads to eternal life with Jesus. And there is a correlation between denying Jesus and the loss of eternity. Such lack of faith leads to behaviors that harm others. Continued denial of Jesus becomes prominent in people's lives that inherently displays a lack of any saving faith ever having been received and thus condemnation for eternity. This is stated clearly in Revelation 21:8 (NIV) *"But the cowardly, the unbelieving, the vile, the murderers, the sexually immoral, those who practice magic arts, the idolaters and all liars—they will be consigned to the fiery lake of burning sulfur. This is the second death."*

Can a person truly say that they are a follower of Jesus and still carry out these reprehensible behaviors? No, not in the way that those behaviors have become the consuming desires of anyone's life. The unbelieving nature leads to vile and evil actions. Followers of Jesus may occasionally err and return to wrong ways; but Jesus working in them brings a change that leads them to repent of these evils and live more in and with Him. However, one without Jesus never looks back to repent.

As Jesus stated in Luke 6:43-44 (NIV) *"A good tree can't produce bad fruit, and a bad tree can't produce good fruit. A tree is identified by its fruit. Figs are never gathered from thornbushes, and grapes are not picked from bramble bushes."* What is at the core of our lives determines our actions and our place in eternity. In the Bible we understand this to mean that we either have a relationship with Jesus established by faith in His grace or we don't. We cannot have eternal life without the Source of life. Light does not come from darkness but from the God of Light. Either we have a faithful relationship with Jesus that will lead to eternal life or we will lose all life in the death of the physical body and the soul apart from God.

By the way, notice back in Revelation 21:8 that such evil people will not have eternal life. Do you think the gracious, fair, loving and just God will have people suffer for eternity if they reject Him? No, He sends them to the fiery lake, the second death of the soul and the body that ends those lives for eternity. This ensures that the people of God never have to deal with the devil, his demons or those unbelievers again in the eternal Kingdom.

The day of Christ's judgment has not yet come upon this world. There is still time for grace from God to be accepted by faith to become a new follower of Jesus. Many around us do not realize that their actions either for or against Jesus in this life move them closer toward or further away from their place in eternity. Let us pray for them to know Jesus as their eternal Savior. This is extremely serious truth to understand. The eternity of death or life depends upon it for each person. Maybe you have not realized this vital truth before in your own life. There is indeed still time to make that decision for yourself. The Lord Jesus would very much love to welcome you into eternal life. Let us all move toward following Jesus more and not away from Him. Let us show everyone that the gracious invitation from Jesus into His eternal Kingdom is still available to all if they too will receive and believe in Him.

As C. S. Lewis wrote *"Here is another thing that used to puzzle me. Is it not frightfully unfair that this new life should be confined to people who have heard of Christ and been able to believe in Him? But the truth is God has not told us what His arrangements about other people are. We do know that no man can be saved except through Christ; we do not know that only those who know Him can be saved through Him. But in the meantime, if you are worried about people outside, the most unreasonable thing you can do is to remain outside yourself. Christians are Christ's body, the organism through which He works. Every addition to that body enables Him to do more. If you want to help those outside you must add your own little cell to the body of Christ who alone can help them. Cutting off a man's fingers would be an odd way of getting him to do more work."* (Mere Christianity, pg. 65)

I truly don't know who all will be in the eternal Kingdom of God. I am glad that I am not the judge of anyone. It is most reassuring to know that Jesus is both fully just and fully merciful. He is the only Savior, yet He is also the only Judge. Only He knows the human heart of each one. Only He knows if a person loves Him in return for His love to them. I am very glad that each of us can know our salvation is assured by our trusting in Jesus to be Savior and Lord. While I don't know who all will be in heaven, there are many that I feel most surely will be there. They display their wonderful love for Jesus openly. I am so grateful for them in the examples they set. May we follow in their footsteps to the heavenly gates and beyond. May we seek the Lord to see His face forever. May we gather to worship Him. May we bring Him glory in great joy from this day and on into eternity. And may we find incredible joy in serving the Lord according to our purpose for eternity. This is my prayer as we trust together in the mercy and promises of our Lord Jesus Christ. And in this great relationship with our loving Lord, may we all look forward to entering into the eternal Kingdom of God with great joy and gladness.

HEAVEN UNVEILED SCRIPTURAL APPENDIX

Chapter 1: Eternal Daylight Time

John 5:24
John 10:10
Philippians 1:21-24
Psalm 39:4
Matthew 6:34
Revelation 22:1-5
1 John 1:5
John 8:12

Chapter 2: Eternal No-Evil Life

Genesis 1:1-2
Isaiah 2:4
Revelation 21:4
Acts 26:18
Revelation 20:10
Romans 8:30
2 Corinthians 3:18
1 Corinthians 15:51-52
Philippians 1:21
Philippians 1:6

Chapter 3: Eternal All-Good Life

1 Corinthians 12:8-12
Isaiah 11:6-9
Matthew 22:30

Michael Paul Clark

Hebrews 8:10-12
Jeremiah 31:31-34
Hebrews 8:12
John 17:3
Ephesians 1:3-10

Chapter 4: Eternal Life Relationships

1 Corinthians 15:51-52
Revelation 6:9
Revelation 7:14-17
Philippians 1:23
2 Corinthians 5:6-8
Luke 16:19-21
Luke 23:43
John 17:3
Revelation 22:3-4
Revelation 4&5
Ephesians 2:19

Chapter 5: Eternal Life Bodies

Philippians 3:20-21
1 Corinthians 15:42-44
1 Corinthians 15:45-49
John 3
1 Corinthians 15:50-52
1 Corinthians 1:13
Luke 22:14-18,29-30
Luke 24:36-43
John 20:19-20
Isaiah 40:31

Chapter 6: Eternal Life Purpose

Revelation 4 & 5
Revelation 5:11-14
Ephesians 2:19
Revelation 22:1-5
Matthew 25:40
James 1:17-18

Chapter 7: Eternal Lifestyle

Matthew 6:9-10
Romans 12:2
Matthew 12:50
Galatians 5:22-23
Ephesians 4:13-15
Romans 8:3
Mark 12:28-34

Chapter 8: Eternal Life Earth

2 Peter 3:10-13
Romans 8:19-21
Revelation 21:1-4
Revelation 7:14-17
Romans 8:20-21
Isaiah 11:6-9

Chapter 9: Eternal Life Dwellings

John 14:2
Revelation 21:10-11
Hebrews 8:5

Revelation 21:12-14
Revelation 21:18-21
Revelation 21:22-27
Joel 3:17
Matthew 6:33-34

Chapter 10: Eternal Life Rewards

Matthew 5:19
Matthew 19:28-30
Matthew 6:1-4
Matthew 16:24-27
1 Corinthians 3:11-15
Matthew 25
Matthew 6:19-21

Chapter 11: Eternal Life Citizens

Matthew 16:27
Matthew 25:31-46
John 1:12
Ephesians 2:8-9
Philippians 2:12-13
James 2:14-17
Revelation 21:8
Luke 6:43-44

ABOUT THE AUTHOR:

Michael P. Clark has pastored for 40 years helping thousands of people in 5 different churches and communities to find new and better life in Christ. He dedicated his life to sharing the life changing truths found in the Bible.

Previous publications by Michael P. Clark include:
* Keep in Step with the Holy Spirit: the Power for Spiritual Renewal in the Church
* Stand Strong! Discover God's Way to Overcome Temptation
* The Marriage Manual: the Bible's Instructions to Build Up Enduring and Healthy Marriages

In addition to the ministry of pastoring churches, the author enjoys scenic photography of the American West with many of his best photos available in large metal formats at his website Inspiringimagespro.com

Made in the USA
Las Vegas, NV
13 July 2024